Something Sweet

100+ GLUTEN-FREE
RECIPES FOR DELICIOUS DESSERTS

LINDSAY GRIMES

weldon**owen**

To jelly boat Joe,
my mom Sharon,
and the two greatest
buns I've ever baked,
Caleb and Nolan.

Contents

Introduction

For most of my life, I thought I was a normal person with a sweet tooth. After writing this book and seeing the way I've obsessed, entangled, and revolved my daily life around getting my next sweet fix, I realize I'm a different kind of normal. Recipe after recipe, I drew from personal stories of a dessert fiend with a one-track mind. That dessert fiend is unapologetically me.

I come from a family of other sweet tooths. Often I'd come home from wherever I was to find my mom relaxing with a bag of chocolate chips. I'd happily join in her nightcap. She was better at savoring each one while I would throw back a handful. I baked alongside her when I was growing up. She taught me that beautifully baked desserts are a way to show love and sweet treats should be a part of our every day, even if it's just a handful of chocolate chips.

As I grew older and the dietary needs of my family changed, I made it one of my top priorities to create recipes that were not only gooey, chocolaty, fudgy, and sink-your-teeth-into delicious, but also were ones that we could all bask in the glory of enjoying together.

As I developed recipes that worked for my family, I found they also struck a chord with others with dietary needs, mainly, the gluten-free community! I love when two people with different eating requirements can indulge and gush over the same dessert without the "GF" designation.

These recipes are exactly that—the all-inclusive and one-and-done desserts that everyone can't wait to eat.

I'm all about making each recipe your own and throughout this book I'll call out substitutions that may work for you and your family. Whether it's subbing in a different nut or seed butter or swapping in dairy-free butter or milk, most of these recipes are flexible to your own personal needs and preferences.

This book is a love letter to sweets. Make them for your loved ones or just for yourself. You deserve it.

Guidelines for This Book

As I developed these recipes, I found myself repeating a few steps over and over. I decided they should be rules for the book—when in doubt, always do this. They are guidelines that I generally live by when I make desserts.

Always cool on a baking sheet

A lot of gluten-free baking, especially with the flours I like, can be quite delicate. I have found that it's best practice to allow things to cool directly on the baking sheet or in the pan. The desserts tend to firm up and really come together in the space between the oven and the cooldown. There's a quiet magic that happens as the sweets cool, giving them strength and sturdiness, and these attributes will only increase your happiness with each bite. I would never tell you to delay dessert enjoyment unless absolutely necessary, so heed this rule as a reminder that patience may, in this case, be worth it.

Always more goodies

I'll always call out how many chocolate chips, sprinkles, and nuts to mix in—things I think of as "goodies." In some recipes, I'll say to reserve some to sprinkle on top because there's nothing like a beautifully baked cookie with pools of melty chocolate to make your taste buds start jumping with joy. If you happen to forget to reserve some toppers, or you just want a bit extra, feel free to grab some more. My general rule of thumb—always more goodies. Whatever the add-in is, grab some extras to press in the top for the "wow" factor.

Flaky salt is your friend

At some point in my foodie life I became obsessed with flaky salt. The sweet and salty combo is nothing new, but the idea that something as small as a pinch could make my treats feel ultra decadent made me reach for my little salt tin whenever I pulled any sweets from the oven. From cookies to brownies, a little pinch goes a long way and is the perfect finisher!

Baking How-Tos

Whether your store ran out of almond flour (or it's ridiculously priced) or you forgot to set out your butter and need it softened perfectly, here are ways to make things run a bit more smoothly when you're baking.

How to make almond flour

INGREDIENTS: 16 oz. raw blanched (skinless) almonds, whole or slivered

PROCESS. Place the almonds in a blender or food processor and turn it on for 30 seconds to 1 minute, until the almonds are a fine, sandy consistency.

SIFT. After you process the almonds, pass them through a sifter into a large bowl so the superfine flour passes through and the bigger pieces are left behind.

REPEAT. Return the bigger pieces left behind after sifting to the blender and process again for 30 seconds to 1 minute. Sift again into the large bowl. Repeat until all the bigger pieces are superfine or the flour reaches your desired consistency. Store in an airtight container and use for recipes.

How to make oat flour

INGREDIENTS: 2 cups gluten free rolled oats

PROCESS. Place the oats in a blender or food processor and turn it on for 30 seconds to 1 minute, until the oats are fine and powdery.

SIFT. After you process the oats, pass them through a sifter into a large bowl so the super-fine flour passes through and the bigger pieces are left behind.

REPEAT. Return the bigger pieces left behind after sifting to the blender and process again for 30 seconds to 1 minute. Sift again into the large bowl. Repeat until all the bigger pieces are superfine or the flour reaches your desired consistency. Store in an airtight container and use for recipes.

How to line a pan with parchment paper

I love lining my baking pans with parchment paper. It not only takes the stress out of excavating your baked good from the pan but also makes for easier cleanup. Over my years of food writing, one thing I've noticed as people recreate my recipes is their struggle with lining their pan. What comes easy to some is crunched and shoved into corners by others. I thought I'd take a quick moment to share how I line my pans with parchment paper for optimal baking and beautiful recipe results.

Generally, I focus on the bottom and two sides of a pan. Lay the parchment so it falls across the bottom neatly and drapes over two sides. To get the parchment to lay flat on the bottom, cut away the excess or fold it underneath.

BREAD PAN AND OTHER RECTANGLE PANS: Focus on cutting the parchment paper so it covers the bottom and two long sides. Sometimes it's helpful to secure the parchment to the pan sides with metal binder clips so the parchment doesn't fall into the batter and affect proper baking. Alternatively, you can crease the parchment along the rim of the pan sides.

SQUARE PAN: This is the same as the bread pan, but because there are no "longer sides," I just lay the parchment across the bottom and drape it over two sides, folding the excess under the bottom so the parchment lies flat. Again, use metal binder clips or crease the parchment along the rim of the pan sides.

ROUND PAN: Set the pan on top of the parchment paper and draw a circle outlining the base of the pan. Use scissors to cut out the circle, making it a little smaller than the drawn circle. Place the circle of parchment on the bottom of the pan.

How to soften butter

INGREDIENTS: 1 stick of butter and 2 cups of water

The glass method

Warm a glass of water in the microwave for 2 minutes until the water is hot. Alternatively, bring the water to a boil on the stove top, then pour it into the glass and let it sit for 30 seconds.

Pour the water into the sink to discard.

Place the glass upside down over a wrapped stick of butter and allow to sit for 10 minutes. The heat from the glass will soften the butter.

The bowl method

Add 2 cups of water to a bowl and microwave for 2 minutes. Alternatively, bring the water to a boil on the stove top, then pour boiling water into the bowl and let it sit for 30 seconds.

Meanwhile, cut the butter into slices and place them in a single layer on a plate that is smaller than the bowl.

Pour the water into the sink to discard.

Place the bowl upside down over the plate and allow it to sit for 10 minutes. The heat from the bowl will soften the butter.

How to melt chocolate

INGREDIENTS: 1–2 cups chocolate chips

The microwave method

Place the chocolate chips in a microwave-safe bowl and microwave for 30 seconds.

Stir the chocolate chips and microwave for another 30 seconds. Continue this process until the chocolate is smooth, thin, and glossy.

The stovetop method

Add 1 inch of water to a pot. Place it over medium-high heat and bring it to a boil.

Once the water is boiling, reduce the heat so the water is a steady simmer.

Add the chocolate to a glass or metal bowl.

Place the bowl on top of the pot and stir the chocolate chips.

Stir the chocolate until smooth.

Baking utensils that make a difference

Cookie scooper

I love using a cookie scooper for even and easy cookie dough balls but if you don't have one, two tablespoons work great! Scoop the batter with one and slide the backside of the second spoon down the first to release the dough onto the pan.

Rubber spatula

While generally I try to dirty as few utensils and dishes in the creation of my desserts (easy clean up!), switching to a rubber spatula at the end of the recipes to fold in your goodies makes for a better dessert. A rubber spatula helps evenly distribute the goodies throughout the batter without overmixing it.

Cookies

In tenth grade, I learned firsthand that cookies have the ability to bring people together. I was seated next to Marci in English class when she pulled out a blue container of mini chocolate chip cookies and started snacking. We began to chat cookies and immediately bonded over our mutual love for the best cookie invention we had ever encountered: the Double Doozie.

The Double Doozie is a cookie sandwich with vanilla frosting nestled in the middle. We gushed about the perfectly chewy cookie and the generous frosting middle. A friendship was born. Time and time again, Marci and I would pull up to the Echelon Mall, beeline to the Great American Cookie Company, and each get a Double Doozie. Marci had the self-control to eat half and save the rest for later. I devoured mine immediately and dealt with the bellyache that came after. Worth it.

Our favorite cookie spot in Echelon has since closed, but Marci travels to a farther location each year for her Double Doozie birthday cake, a tradition I can get behind.

From cookie swaps and holidays to birthday parties and after-school snacks, I can think of any and all reasons to bust out a cookie recipe and start baking. In this chapter you'll find a cookie for every occasion!

After I baked these, I texted my family group chat something along the lines of, "I just made the most amazing cookie, come get some." Turns out, not everyone can drop what they're doing to swing by and impulsively grab cookies. No problem, more for me. The mix of browned butter, roasted cashews, puddles of caramel, and melty chocolate chunks is nothing short of the stuff dreams are made of. And yet, here it is, in real life.

Place the butter in a small saucepan over medium-low heat, stirring constantly until the butter begins to foam and bubble, 5–8 minutes. Once light brown specks form at the bottom of the pan and the butter smells nutty, stop stirring and pour the browned butter into a large bowl. Allow it to cool for about 5 minutes.

Add the coconut sugar, vanilla, and egg to the bowl and whisk until combined. Add the cashew flour, baking soda, and salt. Whisk again until the dry ingredients are incorporated. Fold in most of the chocolate chunks and cashews, saving a few to press into the tops of the cookies before you bake.

Chill the dough in the fridge for 30 minutes.

Preheat the oven to 350°F. Line a baking sheet with parchment paper.

Use a cookie scoop or 2 tablespoons to scoop a cookie dough ball into your hands. Roll it between your hands until smooth and place on the prepared baking sheet. Press a couple chocolate chunks, cashew pieces, and 1 caramel square into the top of each cookie ball. It's okay if the caramel isn't pressed all the way into the ball; it will melt into a gooey puddle on top as it bakes.

Bake for 12 minutes, until the edges are golden brown. Remove the cookies from the oven and allow them to cool on the baking sheet for 10 minutes before sprinkling with flaky salt and transferring to a wire rack.

Chocolate Chunk Cashew Cookies with Caramel Puddles

½ cup unsalted butter

½ cup coconut sugar

1 teaspoon pure vanilla extract

1 egg

1½ cups cashew flour

½ teaspoon baking soda

½ teaspoon salt

½ cup chocolate chunks

½ cup roughly chopped roasted and salted cashews

18 unwrapped caramel squares

Flaky salt for sprinkling

MAKES 18 COOKIES

PREP: 15 MINUTES +
30 MINUTES CHILL TIME
BAKE: 12 MINUTES

Flourless Chocolate Chunk Almond Butter Cookies

1 cup natural almond butter

½ cup coconut sugar

1 teaspoon pure vanilla extract

½ teaspoon baking soda

½ teaspoon salt

2 eggs

½ cup chocolate chunks

MAKES 12 COOKIES
PREP: 10 MINUTES +
30 MINUTES CHILL TIME
BAKE: 10 MINUTES PER BATCH

My brother says that of all the recipes he's tasted for this book, these are his favorite. Me? These recipes are my children, and it would be cruel for me to choose favorites. Having said that, I understand his love. The cookies have a soft, pillowy texture around the edges but are chewy, near gooey in the center. And don't get me started on the beautiful chocolate chunks! Get yourself a glass of milk and grab a few while the chocolate is still melty.

In a large bowl, combine the almond butter, coconut sugar, vanilla, baking soda, salt, and eggs. Use an electric mixer on medium speed to mix together the ingredients until just combined, about 30 seconds. Fold in most of the chocolate chunks, saving some to press into the tops of the cookies.

Chill the dough in the fridge for 30 minutes.

Preheat the oven to 350°F. Line a baking sheet with parchment paper.

Use a cookie scoop or 2 tablespoons to scoop 6 cookie dough balls onto the prepared baking sheet. Press a few reserved chocolate chunks into the top of each ball.

Bake for 10 minutes, until they puff up a bit (they'll deflate as they cool) and the edges appear set. Remove the cookies from the oven and allow them to cool on the baking sheet for about 10 minutes before transferring them to a wire rack or plate. Start on your second batch to use up your remaining cookie dough.

Soft-Baked Oatmeal Snickerdoodle Cookies

½ cup unsalted butter, softened

½ cup coconut sugar

2 eggs

1 teaspoon pure vanilla extract

1½ cups gluten-free rolled oats

1 cup blanched almond flour

2 teaspoons ground cinnamon (divided)

½ teaspoon baking soda

½ teaspoon salt

3 tablespoons turbinado sugar

MAKES 24 COOKIES

PREP: 10 MINUTES +
1 HOUR CHILL TIME
BAKE: 10 MINUTES PER BATCH

Snickerdoodle is quite possibly the cutest name of a baked good ever. *Merriam-Webster* says one of the defining characteristics of a snickerdoodle is that it's rolled in a cinnamon-sugar coating. Mine are happily rolled around in that sweet coating and are also stuffed with hearty, chewy oats. I love using turbinado sugar for the coating because those sugar crystals keep their shape during baking, giving you a beautifully sweet crunch with each bite.

In a large bowl, use an electric mixer on medium speed to combine the butter and coconut sugar. Add the eggs and vanilla and mix again until incorporated. Add the oats, almond flour, 1 teaspoon of cinnamon, the baking soda, and salt and mix again until incorporated.

I like to spread the cookie dough up the sides of the bowl in an even-ish layer to increase the surface area and help the dough chill throughout. Chill in the fridge for about 1 hour.

Preheat the oven to 350°F. Line 2 baking sheets with parchment paper.

In a small bowl, stir together the remaining 1 teaspoon of cinnamon and the turbinado sugar.

Use a cookie scoop or 2 tablespoons to scoop a cookie dough ball into your hands. Roll it in between your hands until smooth and then drop it into the cinnamon-sugar mixture. Roll the cookie dough ball around in the mixture until coated, then place it on the prepared baking sheet. You should be able to fit 12 cookies per baking sheet. Use a couple of fingers or the back of a rubber spatula to lightly press down and flatten the tops of the cookie dough balls.

Bake for 10–12 minutes, until the edges are golden brown. Remove the cookies from the oven and allow them to cool on the baking sheet for about 10 minutes, until the edges firm up and the cookies can easily be picked up.

Cookie dots. Yes, you read that right! Do you remember those colorful dot candies from yesteryear? This recipe is an ode to those but in truth, the only real similarities are they are sweet, small, and arranged in a line. They are perfectly poppable and only moments later, you look down and, oops, you ate the whole batch. It would be adorable to divide the cookie dough into different bowls, add food coloring, and bake these cookie dots in the same style as the original candies. Either way, this recipe lets you have all the dot fun and doesn't require you to ingest paper.

Cinnamon-Sugar Cookie Dots

Preheat the oven to 350°F. Line a baking sheet with parchment paper.

In a medium bowl, whisk together ½ cup of butter, the agave, vanilla, and egg until smooth. Add the oat flour, almond flour, baking powder, and salt. Whisk again until smooth and combined. Allow the dough to sit for 10 minutes to thicken.

Transfer the dough to a piping bag or a zip-top bag and cut off one corner (about ¼ inch). Pipe the cookie dough out onto the prepared baking sheet, making each cookie dot about the size of a nickel and leaving about 1 inch in between the mounds.

Bake for 10 minutes, until the edges are golden brown and the centers are risen and set. Remove the cookies from the oven and allow them to cool on the baking sheet.

Melt the remaining 1 tablespoon of butter in a small bowl in the microwave and set aside. In a medium bowl, stir together the cane sugar and cinnamon. Use a pastry brush to brush the melted butter on top of the cookies, then sprinkle with the cinnamon-sugar mixture.

½ cup + 1 tablespoon unsalted butter, melted (divided)

¼ cup agave nectar, honey, or pure maple syrup

1 teaspoon pure vanilla extract

1 egg

1 cup oat flour

½ cup blanched almond flour

1 teaspoon baking powder

salt

⅓ cup granulated sugar

2 teaspoons ground cinnamon

MAKES 36 COOKIE DOTS

PREP: 20 MINUTES +
10 MINUTES TO SET
BAKE: 10 MINUTES

I went for far too long without tahini in my life. It wasn't something that I drizzled, dipped, or incorporated into my recipes until the last ten years. At some point along the way, I was introduced to halvah—a sweet, sugary sesame treat originating in the Middle East. The sweet plus sesame combo was unreal, and I immediately started using tahini in desserts. If you love sesame, these ultra-rich chocolate chunk tahini cookies will be that recipe you keep in your back pocket! They are crisp around the edges, have a gooey middle, and are rolled in sesame seeds to give that first bite a pop of extra fun.

Preheat the oven to 350°F. Line a baking sheet with parchment paper.

In a medium bowl, whisk together the tahini, agave, vanilla, and egg until combined. Add the almond flour, cocoa powder, baking soda, and salt. Whisk again until combined. The dough should be sticky to the touch. Fold in the chocolate chunks.

Place the sesame seeds in a shallow bowl.

Use a cookie scoop to drop a cookie dough ball into the sesame seeds and roll it around until coated. Roll the ball between your hands to smooth it out and transfer it to the prepared baking sheet. Once you have 12–16 balls on the baking sheet, use your palm or a few fingers to slightly flatten the tops.

Bake for 10 minutes, until the tops are crinkly. Remove the cookies from the oven and allow them to cool on the baking sheet for 2 minutes before transferring them to a wire rack. Make sure to transfer them to the rack. The warm baking sheet will continue to bake the cookies and they'll lose a bit of their chewy, fudgy texture.

Double Chocolate Chunk Tahini Cookies

½ cup tahini

⅓ cup agave nectar

1 teaspoon pure vanilla extract

1 egg

1¼ cups blanched almond flour

2 tablespoons cocoa powder

1 teaspoon baking soda

½ teaspoon salt

½ cup chocolate chunks

¼ cup sesame seeds

MAKES 12–16 COOKIES
PREP: 10 MINUTES
BAKE: 10 MINUTES

Kitchen Sink Cookies

The saying for kitchen sink cookies is they have everything in them but the kitchen sink. In theory, you could just throw in lots of goodies and they'd be delicious. I happily tested a bunch of batches and ate countless cookies to get just the right ratio of sweet, salty, nutty, chewy, and crunchy. Feel free to make these your own with your favorite mix-ins. I've heard of everything from pretzels to potato chips to chopped candies and more! If you can dream it, you can toss it into your kitchen sink cookies.

½ cup unsalted butter, softened

½ cup coconut sugar

1 teaspoon pure vanilla extract

2 eggs

1½ cups blanched almond flour

½ teaspoon baking soda

½ teaspoon salt

½ cup gluten-free rolled oats

½ cup M&M's candies +
more for topping

½ cup chopped pecans

⅓ cup semisweet chocolate chips

⅓ cup peanut butter chips

⅓ cup unsweetened shredded coconut

MAKES 12–16 LARGE COOKIES
PREP: 10 MINUTES
BAKE: 15 MINUTES PER BATCH

Preheat the oven to 350°F. Line a baking sheet with parchment paper.

In a large bowl, whisk together the butter, coconut sugar, vanilla, and eggs. Add the almond flour, baking soda, and salt. Whisk again until combined. Now, throw in all the goodies—the oats, M&M's, pecans, chocolate and peanut butter chips, and coconut. Use a rubber spatula to fold it all together.

Use a large cookie scoop to scoop 6–8 large mounds onto the prepared baking sheet. Add additional M&M's to the top of each cookie dough ball.

Bake for 15 minutes, until the cookies puff up and are golden brown around the edges. Although they may appear puffy out of the oven, they'll deflate and become chewier as they cool. While the cookies are baking, prep the second batch.

Remove the cookies from the oven and allow them to cool completely on the baking sheet before transferring to a serving plate.

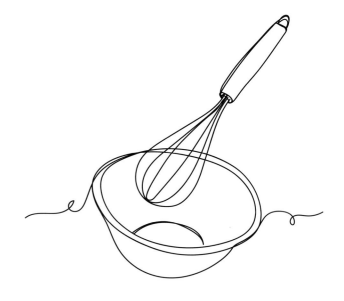

My kids went through a phase of grabbing those Lofthouse cookies whenever we were at the grocery store. I don't remember them ten-plus years ago, but maybe I was too focused on Nutella? Suddenly, Lofthouse cookies are in every color for every holiday and line up to greet you when you enter the grocery store door. I decided to convert my wee children with a similar style soft-baked, cakey cookie topped with colorful frosting and sprinkles. Mission accomplished.

To make the cookies, preheat the oven to 350°F. Line a baking sheet with parchment paper.

In a large bowl, use an electric mixer on medium-high speed to cream together the butter, agave, vanilla, and egg until combined, about 1 minute. Add the almond flour, oat flour, baking powder, and salt. Mix again until combined.

Use a cookie scoop to drop 12 cookie dough balls onto the prepared baking sheet. Dampen your hands and tuck in any cookie dough that's sticking out and flatten the tops of the cookie dough balls.

Bake for 12 minutes, until the edges are golden brown. Remove the cookies from the oven and allow them to cool on the baking sheet for a few minutes before transferring them to a wire rack to cool completely.

Once the cookies are cool, make the frosting. In a medium bowl, use an electric mixer on high speed to cream together the powdered sugar, butter, cream, and vanilla until light and fluffy, about 3 minutes. Add the food coloring, then mix until evenly incorporated.

Transfer the frosting to a piping bag or a zip-top bag and cut off one corner (about ½ inch). Pipe the frosting onto the cooled cookies in a circular motion. Finish the cookies with sprinkles.

Frosted Fluffy Vanilla Cake Cookies

FOR THE COOKIES

⅓ cup unsalted butter, softened

⅓ cup agave nectar, honey, or pure maple syrup

1 teaspoon pure vanilla extract

1 egg

1 cup blanched almond flour

½ cup oat flour

1 teaspoon baking powder

½ teaspoon salt

FOR THE FROSTING

1 cup powdered sugar

4 tablespoons unsalted butter

1 tablespoon heavy cream

1 teaspoon pure vanilla extract

Couple drops food coloring of choice

Rainbow sprinkles for decorating

MAKES 12 COOKIES
PREP: 15 MINUTES
BAKE: 12 MINUTES

Chewy Cashew Butter Sprinkle Cookies

½ cup natural cashew butter

⅓ cup agave nectar

1 teaspoon pure vanilla extract

1 egg

1½ cups blanched almond flour

1 teaspoon baking soda

½ teaspoon sea salt

Rainbow sprinkles for decorating

MAKES 16 COOKIES
PREP: 10 MINUTES
BAKE: 10 MINUTES PER BATCH

Don't you dare tell me you didn't smile when you saw those colorful sprinkles. You monster! They're happy, they're fun, and they're perfect for any and every occasion! What I love most about these sprinkle cookies is they have a cashew butter base, making for a super-soft, chewy texture. Cashew butter can taste more or less like cashews, depending on the brand, so make sure to find one that suits your preferences.

Preheat the oven to 350°F. Line a baking sheet with parchment paper.

In a large bowl, whisk together the cashew butter, agave, vanilla, and egg and whisk until combined. Add the almond flour, baking soda, and sea salt. Whisk again until combined.

Use an ice cream scoop to scoop a large cookie dough ball into your hands and roll it between your hands until smooth.

Spread the sprinkles out on a plate or shallow bowl in a single layer. Roll each cookie dough ball around until it's completely covered with sprinkles. Place it on the prepared baking sheet. You'll end up with about 8 balls.

Bake for 10 minutes, until the edges are golden brown. Transfer to a wire rack and continue on to make your next batch.

Double Chocolate Coconut Macaroons

4 egg whites

½ cup agave nectar, honey, or pure maple syrup

¼ cup cocoa powder

¼ teaspoon salt

3 cups unsweetened shredded coconut

½ cup semisweet chocolate chips

2 tablespoons refined coconut oil

Flaky salt for sprinkling

MAKES 24 MACAROONS
PREP: 10 MINUTES
BAKE: 15 MINUTES

If you ever need to know how much I love macaroons, just picture a super-pregnant Lindsay walking out of a Philadelphia bakery with a satisfied smile and an enormous macaroon in her hand. Damn the wax paper that made it slip from my grip and fall onto the filthy Philly street! Without hesitating, I picked it up, brushed it off, and was fully prepared to take a bite until my husband intervened. I've thought about that lost macaroon in the years since, and I have made it my life's mission to create a homemade version good enough to warrant a three-second rule kind of loyalty. Enjoy!

Preheat the oven to 350°F. Line 2 baking sheets with parchment paper.

Place the egg whites in a medium bowl and use an electric mixer on high speed to mix for about 3 minutes, until the egg whites stiffen. Add the agave, cocoa powder, and salt. Mix again for a few seconds to incorporate into the egg whites. Add the coconut and use a rubber spatula to incorporate.

Use a cookie scoop to scoop 12 mounds onto each prepared baking sheet. Use your fingers to tuck in any stray coconut that sticks out.

Bake for 15 minutes, until the edges are slightly browned. Remove the cookies from the oven and allow them to cool on the baking sheet.

In a small bowl, melt the chocolate chips in the microwave, stirring every 30 seconds until smooth. (Alternatively, use a double boiler.) Whisk in the coconut oil to help thin it out a bit.

Use a fork to lower each macaroon into the chocolate to coat the bottom, then place it back on the parchment paper. Once all have been dipped, drizzle any additional chocolate on the tops and sprinkle with flaky salt.

Chill in the fridge for 5–10 minutes, until the chocolate hardens. Store in an airtight container at room temperature for up to 7 days.

My kids aren't big coconut fans (yet—I still have hope). It's shocking to me because, as far back as I remember, I was reaching for Almond Joys every time I saw one (if you're the same, you'll love the recipe on page 146). Maybe there are coconut people and non-coconut people. If you're one of the latter, please, please step aside for this one. These coconut cookies are toasty, crisp, and dipped in chocolate to finish them off. Whatever you do, make sure you allow them to cool on the pan *completely* before touching them! Don't say I didn't warn you!

Preheat the oven to 350°F. Line a baking sheet with parchment paper.

In a medium bowl, combine the coconut, coconut flour, and salt. Add the coconut oil and agave. Mix everything until it's combined.

Form little cookie discs, about 2 inches in diameter, and place them on the prepared baking sheet.

Bake for 12 minutes, until the edges are slightly golden brown and toasty. Remove the cookies from the oven and allow them to cool completely on the baking sheet before transferring them to a wire rack.

In a small bowl, melt the chocolate in the microwave, stirring every 30 seconds until smooth. (Alternatively, use a double boiler.) Dip each cookie halfway into the chocolate. Place it back on the wire rack or on a piece of parchment paper.

Chocolate-Dipped Coconut Cookies

1 cup unsweetened shredded coconut

¼ cup coconut flour

½ teaspoon salt

¼ cup refined coconut oil, melted

¼ cup agave nectar, honey, or pure maple syrup

2 oz chocolate

MAKES 12 COOKIES

PREP: 10 MINUTES
BAKE: 12 MINUTES

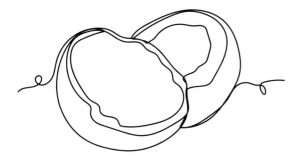

To the genius who invented slice 'n' bake cookies, I think about you often. The beauty of laying in bed at night knowing a luxurious log of cookie dough is waiting patiently in your freezer is a joy everyone should know at one point in their lives. One reader told me she makes herself a log of cookie dough and slices off a cookie each night to bake and enjoy after a long day's work. I've never admired someone more. These salted brown butter pecan cookies make your taste buds dance. They have that rich, caramelly brown butter base and are loaded with chopped nuts, making them a ringer for Pecan Sandies.

Place the butter in a small saucepan over medium-low heat, stirring constantly until the butter begins to foam and bubble, 5–8 minutes. Once light brown specks form at the bottom of the pan and the butter smells nutty, stop stirring and pour the browned butter into a large bowl. Allow it to cool for about 5 minutes.

Add the agave, coconut sugar, and vanilla to the bowl, then whisk until smooth. Use a rubber spatula to fold in the almond flour, pecans, and salt until the dough comes together.

Lay a piece of plastic wrap out on a cutting board. Transfer the cookie dough to the center of the plastic wrap. Use the rubber spatula to form the dough into a log. The cookie dough can be sticky, so I lift the sides of the plastic wrap to help form an even log.

Fold the plastic wrap around the log, add another piece of plastic wrap if needed, and freeze for 12 hours or up to overnight. When you're ready for some cookies, preheat the oven to 350°F. Line a baking sheet with parchment paper.

Unwrap the cookie dough log slices and place on the prepared and place it on a cutting board. Use a sharp knife to cut into ½-inch slices and place on the prepared baking sheet. The cookies don't expand too much so you should be able to fit 12 cookies on a sheet comfortably.

Bake for 15–18 minutes, until the centers no longer look wet and the edges look set. These cookies really firm up on the pan. Remove the cookies from the oven. Sprinkle them with flaky salt and allow them to cool on the baking sheet for 10–15 minutes.

Salted Brown Butter Pecan Slice 'n' Bake Cookies

6 tablespoons unsalted butter

¼ cup agave nectar, honey, or pure maple syrup

¼ cup coconut sugar

1 teaspoon pure vanilla extract

2 cups blanched almond flour

½ cup chopped pecans

½ teaspoon salt

Flaky salt for sprinkling

MAKES 12 COOKIES

PREP: 15 MINUTES +
12 HOURS CHILL TIME

BAKE: 15 MINUTES

Shortbread Cutout Cookies

Shape cookies are always a fun recipe to have at the ready, whether you're making a cookie plate for the holidays or just want a fun activity with kids. This recipe is the same as the Vanilla Berry Linzer Cookies (page 36), but instead of making juicy jammy sandwiches, we're decorating them with sweet icing. My icing skills leave a lot to be desired, but don't let your lack of expertise stunt your fun. Be mindful of how much milk you add—you don't want the icing to be too drippy (or do you?).

FOR THE COOKIES

6 tablespoons unsalted butter, softened

¼ cup agave nectar, honey, or pure maple syrup

1 teaspoon pure vanilla extract

2 cups blanched almond flour

½ teaspoon salt

FOR THE ICING

1 cup powdered sugar

2 tablespoons agave nectar, honey, or pure maple syrup

½–1 tablespoon whole milk, plus more as needed

½ teaspoon pure vanilla extract

Couple drops food coloring of choice

MAKES 12 LARGE COOKIES

PREP: 10 MINUTES +
30 MINUTES CHILL TIME
BAKE: 10 MINUTES

To make the cookies, in a large bowl, whisk together the butter, agave, and vanilla. Add the almond flour and salt. Whisk again until combined.

Place the dough between 2 large pieces of parchment paper and roll it out to a ⅛-inch thickness. Slide a cutting board or baking sheet under the bottom parchment paper and freeze the dough for 30 minutes. The key to this recipe is working with the dough when it's super cold, so make sure to chill the dough for at least 30 minutes.

Preheat the oven to 350°F. Line a baking sheet with parchment paper.

Remove the dough from the freezer. Peel off the top layer of parchment paper and discard it. Use a cookie cutter of your choice to cut 12 cookies from the dough and place them on the prepared baking sheet. This recipe works best with a cookie cutter that isn't too intricate. Use a butter knife to slide under the cut cookie and transfer it to the baking sheet.

Bake for 10–12 minutes, until the edges are golden brown and the centers are still a light shortbread color. Remove the cookies from the oven and allow them to cool completely on the baking sheet.

To make the icing, in a small bowl, whisk together the powdered sugar, agave, milk, and vanilla until incorporated. You want it to be thick so it doesn't run when you pipe it. Add more milk as needed. Divide into separate bowls, depending on how many colors you are using. Add a drop or two of food coloring to your bowls.

Transfer the icing to piping bags or zip-top bags and cut off one corner of each (about ⅛ inch). Pipe the icing as desired onto your cookies to decorate them.

I was scrolling Instagram one day and saw someone post about cookie corners. They went abroad and saw these triangle-shaped cookies a bakery had adorably dubbed "cookie corners." It's like when your mom cuts your sandwich down the middle your whole life, and then one day, she cuts on a diagonal. It feels bold, it feels revolutionary, and it gives your lunch box a whole new look. Circle cookies will be my forever favorite, but there are always days when you need the thrill of the diagonal.

To make the cookies, preheat the oven to 350°F. Line a 9-inch square baking pan with parchment paper.

In a large bowl, whisk together the butter, agave, vanilla, and egg. Add the almond and oat flours, baking powder, and salt. Whisk again until combined.

Transfer the batter to the prepared pan and use a rubber spatula to smooth the batter out in an even layer.

Bake for 25 minutes, until the edges are golden brown and the center is set. Remove the shortbread from the oven and allow it to cool completely.

Now it's time to cut them into corners! Use a butter knife to slide between the shortbread and the pan. Pull the edges of the parchment paper to lift the shortbread from the pan and place it on a cutting board. Cut 9 squares, then cut each square on a diagonal to make right triangle cookie corners. I find it easiest to place the cookie corners on a wire rack on top of a lined baking sheet to collect the icing when it falls.

To make the icing, in a medium bowl, whisk together the powdered sugar, 2 tablespoons of milk, the vanilla, and coconut oil.

Use a spoon to cover half of each cookie with vanilla icing. Add the cocoa powder and remaining 1 teaspoon of milk to the leftover vanilla icing. Whisk until smooth.

Use a spoon to cover the other half of each cookie with chocolate icing, making a black-and-white cookie triangle.

Transfer the whole tray to the fridge to allow the icing to set, about 30 minutes. These cookie corners are best served at room temperature.

Black-and-White Shortbread Cookie Corners

FOR THE COOKIES

⅓ cup unsalted butter, melted and cooled

⅓ cup agave nectar, honey, or pure maple syrup

1 teaspoon pure vanilla extract

1 egg

1 cup blanched almond flour

½ cup oat flour

1 teaspoon baking powder

½ teaspoon salt

FOR THE ICING

1 cup confectioners' sugar, sifted

2 tablespoons + 1 teaspoon whole milk (divided)

½ teaspoon pure vanilla extract

1 tablespoon refined coconut oil, melted

1 teaspoon cocoa powder

MAKES 18 COOKIES
PREP: 15 MINUTES
BAKE: 25 MINUTES

Vanilla Berry Linzer Cookies

When I first found out about Linzer cookies I was disappointed. It may sound silly, but I felt a dessert whose name so closely resembled my own would surely be drenched in chocolate, no? Eventually, I gave in and was delighted by the cookies' delicate shortbread and fruity centers. They opened my eyes to the possibility that fruity confections should be met with an embrace and not an eye roll. These cookie sandwiches have the perfect soft and buttery texture with a pop of juicy jam in the center. I use my favorite shortbread cookie recipe here, which can be enjoyed on its own, cut into fun shapes, dipped in chocolate, or topped with rainbow sprinkles. Customize the fruity flavor by swapping the berry jam for orange, apricot, fig, or even Nutella!

6 tablespoons unsalted butter, softened

¼ cup agave nectar, honey, or pure maple syrup

1 teaspoon pure vanilla extract

2 cups blanched almond flour

½ teaspoon salt

⅓ cup berry jam

Powdered sugar for dusting

MAKES 12 COOKIE SANDWICHES

PREP: 20 MINUTES +
30 MINUTES CHILL TIME
BAKE: 8 MINUTES PER BATCH

In a large bowl, whisk together the butter, agave, and vanilla. Add the almond flour and salt. Whisk again until combined.

Sandwich the dough between 2 pieces of parchment paper and roll it out to a ⅛-inch thickness. Slide a cutting board or baking sheet under the bottom parchment paper and freeze the dough for 30 minutes. The key to this recipe is working with the dough when it's super cold, so make sure to chill the dough for at least 30 minutes.

Preheat the oven to 350°F. Line a baking sheet with parchment paper.

Use a 2-inch circle cookie cutter to cut 12 cookies from the dough and place them on the prepared baking sheet. I find it easiest to use a butter knife to slide under the cut cookie and transfer it to the baking sheet.

Gather up the scraps and reroll out the remaining dough between the 2 pieces of parchment paper and place it back in the freezer before cutting the second batch.

Bake for about 8 minutes, until the edges are golden brown and the centers are still a light shortbread color. Remove the cookies from the oven and allow them to cool on the baking sheet for 5 minutes before transferring them to a wire rack. If you try to move them too soon, they could fall apart.

Continues on page 38

Continued from page 36

Make sure the dough for the second batch is chilled enough to work with. Use the same circle cookie cutter to cut out another 12 cookies. Use a smaller shape cutter to cut out a cute design in the center of the cookie. Slide the butter knife under the cut cookie and transfer it to the baking sheet.

Bake the second batch for 8 minutes. Remove the cookies from the oven and allow them to cool on the baking sheet for 5 minutes, then transfer them to a wire rack to cool completely.

To assemble the sandwiches, spread some jam across the bottom of a solid cookie, then place a cookie with a cutout center, bottom side down, on top of the jam.

I remember going to my cousin's house around Christmas when I was young, and her mom had a little bowl of wrapped chocolates on the counter. I pulled up a stool and started fishing for the milk chocolates. I asked my cousin if she wanted one and she declined, claiming to only like white chocolate. I couldn't wrap my head around the idea of not liking all the different kinds of chocolate. After my initial shock, I realized that meant more for me and let her have all the white chocolates. These cookies have silky white chocolate chunks that play perfectly off the tangy raspberries. I use freeze-dried fruit here because it doesn't add extra moisture like fresh fruit would. Play around with different fruit to switch it up!

In a medium bowl, melt the butter in the microwave. Add the coconut sugar, vanilla, and egg. Whisk until combined. Add the almond flour, oats, baking soda, and salt. Whisk again until combined. Fold in most of the white chocolate and most of the raspberries, saving some to top the cookies.

Chill the dough in the fridge for 30 minutes to 1 hour.

Preheat the oven to 350°F. Line a baking sheet with parchment paper.

Use a cookie scoop to scoop out 2-tablespoon cookie dough balls on the prepared baking sheet. Press the remaining white chocolate into the tops of the balls and flatten the tops slightly.

Bake for 10–12 minutes, until the edges are golden brown. Remove the cookies from the oven and allow them to cool on the baking sheet for 15 minutes.

With the back of a spoon or fork, crush the remaining freeze-dried raspberries. They don't have to be too powdery, just smaller pieces. Sprinkle the tops of the cookies with the crushed raspberries and flaky salt.

Raspberry and White Chocolate Chunk Cookies

½ cup unsalted butter

½ cup coconut sugar

1 teaspoon pure vanilla extract

1 egg

1 cup blanched almond flour

1 cup gluten-free rolled oats

½ teaspoon baking soda

½ teaspoon salt

4 oz white chocolate, roughly chopped

½ cup freeze-dried raspberries

Flaky salt for sprinkling

MAKES 18 COOKIES

PREP: 10 MINUTES +
30 MINUTES CHILL TIME
BAKE: 10 MINUTES

As a love letter to my favorite peanut cookie, I've created my own soft-baked version that rivals any whoopie pie or peanut cookie around. They are adorably shaped like peanuts (wait for the aahs from the crowd) and melt in your mouth with soft peanut buttery charm.

To make the cookies, in a medium bowl, whisk together the peanut butter, agave, vanilla, and egg until combined. Add the almond flour, oat flour, baking soda, and salt. Whisk again until combined.

Place the dough in the freezer and chill for about 30 minutes. The batter is pretty sticky, so freezing it will help it firm up and be easier to handle. I've tried chilling this in the fridge, but it just doesn't do the trick.

Preheat the oven to 350°F. Line a baking sheet with parchment paper.

With damp hands, roll ½–1 teaspoon of cookie dough into a marble-size ball. Place it on the prepared baking sheet. Make a second marble-size cookie dough ball and place it touching the first. Continue this process to create pairs of touching balls, spacing each pair about 1 inch apart. With damp fingers, pat down each pair into a flat peanut shape.

Bake for 10–12 minutes, until the cookies rise. Remove the cookies from the oven and allow them to cool on the baking sheet for a few minutes before transferring them to a wire rack. Continue with a second batch until the cookie dough is used up.

To make the filling, while the cookies are are cooling, in a small bowl, stir together the peanut butter and agave. Transfer the filling to a piping bag or a zip-top bag and cut off one corner (about ½ inch). Once the cookies are cool, pipe the peanut butter filling onto the bottom of 1 cookie. Then place another cookie, bottom side down, on top of the filling to make a sandwich. You should get about 14 sandwiches.

Enjoy these immediately. Store in an airtight container at room temperature for 3 days or in the fridge for about 1 week.

Soft-Baked Peanut Sandos

FOR THE COOKIES

½ cup natural peanut butter

¼ cup agave nectar, honey, or pure maple syrup

1 teaspoon pure vanilla extract

1 egg

⅓ cup blanched almond flour

2 tablespoons oat flour

½ teaspoon baking soda

¼ teaspoon salt

FOR THE FILLING

⅓ cup natural peanut butter

2 tablespoons agave nectar, honey, or pure maple syrup

MAKES 14 COOKIE SANDWICHES

PREP: 20 MINUTES +
30 MINUTES CHILL TIME
BAKE: 10 MINUTES PER BATCH

Soft Chocolate Whoopie Pies with Vanilla Buttercream

When I was about seven, I became obsessed with Swiss rolls. You know, that chocolate cake pastry swirled around silky white frosting? My goal for these whoopie pies was to capture the chocolaty cake flavor of those traditional Swiss rolls and pair it with a vanilla buttercream that could stand its ground. Have whoopie pies replaced Swiss rolls in my heart? Never! My heart only expands. But "whoopie" is quite fun to say.

FOR THE COOKIES

4 tablespoons unsalted butter, melted

½ cup coconut sugar

1 teaspoon pure vanilla extract

2 eggs

½ cup blanched almond flour

¼ cup oat flour

¼ cup cocoa powder

½ teaspoon baking powder

¼ teaspoon salt

FOR THE BUTTERCREAM FILLING

¼ cup heavy cream

½ teaspoon arrowroot flour

½ cup cold unsalted butter, cubed

¼ cup agave nectar, honey, or pure maple syrup

1 teaspoon pure vanilla extract

¼ teaspoon salt

MAKES 6–8 COOKIES
PREP: 20 MINUTES
BAKE: 12 MINUTES PER BATCH

To make the cookies, preheat the oven to 350°F. Line a baking sheet with parchment paper.

In a large bowl, whisk together the butter, coconut sugar, vanilla, and eggs. Add the almond flour, oat flour, cocoa powder, baking powder, and salt. Whisk again until the dry ingredients are incorporated. Allow the batter to sit for 5 minutes to thicken.

Use a cookie scoop to scoop 6–8 cookies onto the prepared baking sheet.

Bake for 12 minutes, until the cookies look fluffy and set on the top and edges. Remove the cookies from the oven and allow them to cool on the baking sheet for 1–2 minutes before transferring them to a wire rack. Start on a second batch of cookies.

To make the buttercream filling, while the cookies are cooling, combine the cream and arrowroot flour in a small pan over medium heat. Whisk constantly for 30 seconds to 1 minute, until the mixture thickens. Remove the pan from the heat and set aside to cool for 5 minutes. This may be a weird way to make buttercream, but trust me on this!

Continues on page 44

Continued from page 42

Place the butter, agave, vanilla, and salt in the bowl of a stand mixer. Mix on medium speed until creamed together, about 1 minute. Add the cooled cream mixture and mix on high until it lightens and is fluffy. If it looks like it's separating, stop to scrape down the sides and mix again on high. It should come together within about 2 minutes. Make sure not to overmix!

Transfer the buttercream to a piping bag or a zip-top bag and cut off one corner (about ½ inch). Once the chocolate cookies are completely cooled, pipe the buttercream out in a circular motion on the bottom of one cookie, then place a second cookie, bottom side down, on top of the buttercream to make a sandwich. Continue this process to make 6–8 sandwiches.

These are best eaten immediately or store them in an airtight container at room temperature for about 2 days.

When I was younger, my mom put together a binder of some of my grandmom Anne's favorite recipes. I revisited that binder as I was drafting ideas for this book and stopped dead in my tracks when I saw "Butter Balls" written across the top of a recipe card. Surely butter balls had to be a winner. As I read through the recipe, I realized these were the same cookie (among dozens of others) that my mom made every year at Christmas. Some call them snowballs or Mexican wedding cookies, but for me, Butter Balls is the perfect description. Here, I update my grandmom's recipe with agave and almond flour in lieu of traditional sugar and flour.

Preheat the oven to 350°F. Line 2 baking sheets with parchment paper.

In a large bowl, use a rubber spatula to mix together the butter, agave, and vanilla. Add the almond flour and mix until combined. Add the walnuts and mix until they are evenly distributed throughout the dough.

Use a cookie scoop to make a 2-tablespoon-size ball. Roll it between your hands until smooth and place it on the prepared baking sheet. You should be able to fit 12 balls per baking sheet.

Bake each batch for 15 minutes, until the tops of the balls turn the slightest bit golden brown. Remove the cookie balls from the oven, transfer them to a wire rack, and allow them to cool completely. Adding the powdered sugar too soon, when the cookies are too warm, will make the sugar melt and turn a bit slimy (as my nephew put it).

Place the powdered sugar in a large bowl or a large zip-top bag. Place a few balls in the bowl and swirl around (or shake them in the bag) until they are coated with the powdered sugar. Transfer to a serving dish.

Walnut Butter Balls

4 tablespoons unsalted butter, melted

⅓ cup agave nectar, honey, or pure maple syrup

1 teaspoon pure vanilla extract

2 cups blanched almond flour

1 cup chopped walnuts

½ cup sifted powdered sugar

MAKES 24 COOKIES

PREP: 10 MINUTES
BAKE: 15 MINUTES PER BATCH

Brownies & Bars

Pretty much weekly throughout middle school and early high school, my friends and I would go to dinner and a movie. The movie theater was right next to TGI Fridays, and we'd pop from one to the other seamlessly. My priority was obviously dessert. Their brownie sundae was the perfect mix of warm, gooey chocolate and cold, melty ice cream and hot fudge. Time and time again, I'd march into that Fridays, and my mouth would immediately water in some Pavlovian response, anticipating the first scrumptious chocolaty bite.

That brownie sundae imprinted on me at a young age and became the gold standard to which I measured all brownies thereafter. As my taste buds became more, ahem, mature, I realized other desserts, too, had value. I not only saw merit in other chocolate treats but also learned to appreciate the fruity, the buttery, and all desserts of any form, really.

In this chapter, you'll find (yes) fudgy, gooey brownies you won't be able to stop thinking about. But you'll also find squares and bars of all flavors that are just as dreamy.

Strawberry Cheesecake Swirl Brownies

The mix of intense, fudgy brownies and a creamy, fruity swirl just knocks this dessert out of the park. The brownie base is swirled with a luscious strawberry cheesecake batter to create a beautiful marbled effect.

FOR THE BROWNIE LAYER

1½ cups chocolate chips
of choice, melted and cooled

½ cup coconut sugar

¼ cup agave nectar

1 teaspoon pure vanilla extract

2 eggs

1 egg yolk

1 cup blanched almond flour

¼ cup cocoa powder

½ teaspoon salt

FOR THE CHEESECAKE LAYER

8 oz cream cheese, room temperature

1 cup frozen strawberries, thawed

3 tablespoons agave nectar

½ teaspoon pure vanilla extract

MAKES 9 BROWNIES

PREP: 15 MINUTES
BAKE: 35 MINUTES

To make the brownie layer, preheat the oven to 350°F. Line an 8-inch square pan with parchment paper so that it lines the bottom and drapes over two sides of the pan.

In a large bowl, whisk together the chocolate, coconut sugar, agave, vanilla, eggs, and egg yolk until smooth. Add the almond flour, cocoa powder, and salt. Whisk again until combined and set aside.

To make the cheesecake layer, in a medium bowl, use a clean whisk to combine the cream cheese, strawberries, agave, and vanilla until smooth.

Pour most of the brownie batter into the prepared pan and use a rubber spatula to spread it into the edges and corners. Pour the cheesecake batter on top of the brownie layer and spread it out. Use a spoon to dollop the remaining brownie batter on top of the cheesecake layer. Use a toothpick or chopstick to create swirls in the brownie dollops and cheesecake layer.

Bake for 35 minutes, until the top puffs up and the edges appear set. Remove the brownie from the oven and allow it to cool for 15 minutes. Slide a knife around the sides where the brownie touches the pan, then pull the edges of the parchment paper to lift everything from the pan and place it on a cutting board. Cut into 9 squares.

My mom and I decided that since this is made of almonds and fruit, it's basically a healthy meal you can eat any time of day, breakfast included. If you love the traditional flavors of a cherry pie but don't want to fuss with the crimping and pinching of an actual pie, these bars will answer all your prayers. Switch up the filling with whatever fruit you have stashed away in your freezer. Peaches, mixed berries, or even a tropical mango would be delicious. Enjoy the bars as is or serve them alongside a scoop of vanilla ice cream.

Cherry Pie Shortbread Crumble Bars

To make the shortbread crust, preheat the oven to 350°F. Line an 8-inch square pan with parchment paper so that it lines the bottom and drapes over two sides of the pan.

In a large bowl, use a rubber spatula to mix together the almond flour, coconut oil, agave, vanilla, and salt. Place about two-thirds of the shortbread mixture into the prepared pan and press it into the bottom and corners to make an even layer.

Bake for 10–12 minutes, until the edges are golden brown (but keep the oven on).

To make the cherry filling, while the shortbread bakes, combine the cherries, water, lemon zest, lemon juice, and agave in a medium saucepan over medium-high heat. Use a spatula to stir and press some of the cherries to break them down a little bit. Cook for about 10 minutes, until the cherries are softened and broken apart and the liquid is thicker and reduced.

When the shortbread is finished baking, spread the cherry mixture on top. Using your hands, crumble the remaining shortbread mixture on top of the cherry layer.

Bake for another 10 minutes, until the top crumbles are golden brown. Remove the pan from the oven and allow the bars to cool to room temperature. If you're prepping these ahead, they'll set really well in the pan covered in the fridge.

Slide a knife around the sides where the bars touch the pan, then pull the edges of the parchment paper to lift everything from the pan and place it on a cutting board. Cut into 12 squares. Store in the fridge in an airtight container for about 1 week.

FOR THE CRUST

4 cups blanched almond flour

¾ cup refined coconut oil

⅓ cup agave nectar

1½ teaspoons pure vanilla extract

1 teaspoon salt

FOR THE CHERRY FILLING

16 oz frozen pitted cherries

¼ cup water

1 tablespoon grated lemon zest

¼ cup fresh lemon juice

2 tablespoons agave nectar

MAKES 12 BARS
PREP: 20 MINUTES
BAKE: 20 MINUTES

Raspberry Cheesecake Bars with a Pecan Crust

I love the combination of juicy raspberries and silky-smooth cheesecake. Add in the buttery, nutty texture of the pecan crust and you are set with the perfect contrast of flavors and textures. These bars are easy to put together and can be prepped in advance, making them super convenient for any occasion!

FOR THE CRUST

2 cups raw pecans

1 cup blanched almond flour

2 tablespoons coconut sugar

½ teaspoon salt

2 tablespoons natural almond butter

4 tablespoons unsalted butter, melted

FOR THE CHEESECAKE

16 oz cream cheese, room temperature

2 eggs

¼ cup + 1 tablespoon agave nectar, honey, or pure maple syrup (divided)

1 teaspoon pure vanilla extract

6 oz fresh raspberries

MAKES 16 BARS

PREP: 15 MINUTES +
2 HOURS CHILL TIME
BAKE: 50 MINUTES

To make the crust, preheat the oven to 350°F. Line a 9-inch square pan with parchment paper.

Place the pecans, almond flour, coconut sugar, and salt in a food processor and process for about 20 seconds, until chopped up into a chunky meal. Add the almond butter and butter and pulse again until the dough balls up and is tacky to the touch.

Transfer the dough into the prepared pan and use your fingers to press it down in an even layer. If you're having trouble working with it, dampen your hands so it doesn't stick. Set aside.

To make the cheesecake, in a medium bowl, combine the cream cheese, eggs, ¼ cup of agave nectar, and the vanilla. Use an electric mixer on medium speed to cream the ingredients together until smooth, about 2 minutes.

Add most of the raspberries to the cream cheese mixture and mix again until the raspberries are incorporated and the cream cheese mixture turns pink. Transfer it to the top of the crust and smooth it out in an even layer.

In a small bowl, combine the remaining raspberries and 1 tablespoon of agave. Use a fork to mash and mix the ingredients together. Use a spoon to dollop the raspberry mixture on top of the cream cheese layer. Use a toothpick or butter knife to slide through the dollops to create swirls on top of the cheesecake.

Bake for 50–55 minutes, until the edges are golden brown and the center is only slightly jiggly. Remove the cheesecake from the oven and allow it to cool to room temperature. Chill in the fridge for at least 2 hours. Cut into 16 squares.

Caramel apples confuse me. Sure, they are pretty, but are you supposed to hold the stick and bite right into them? Cut them up and share them? What happens when inevitably you bite off all the caramel and are left with just an apple? This recipe is my answer to the problem nobody has had but me. I'm distributing the sweet caramel apple into every bite and saving your teeth in the process.

To make the crust, preheat the oven to 350°F. Line an 8-inch square pan with parchment paper so that it lines the bottom and drapes over two sides of the pan.

In a large bowl, whisk together the almond flour, butter, agave, vanilla, and salt. It may be easier to use a rubber spatula to fold the ingredients together until combined if the whisk gets a bit too clumpy. Transfer three-fourths of the dough to the prepared pan. Use your hands to press it down in an even layer in the bottom.

Bake for 10 minutes, until the edges are golden brown. Remove the crust from the oven (but keep the oven on).

To make the caramel apple filling, in a large saucepan over high heat, combine the butter, agave, coconut sugar, vanilla, cinnamon, salt, arrowroot flour, and apple cubes. Bring to a rolling boil and cook for 15–20 minutes, until the apples are tender and the caramel syrup around the fruit reduces.

Pour the apple mixture on top of the baked crust and spread it out in an even layer. Crumble the remaining crust dough on top of the caramel mixture.

Bake for 10–12 minutes, until the top crumbles are golden brown. Remove the bars from the oven and allow them to cool to room temperature.

Slide a knife around the sides where the bars touch the pan, then pull the edges of the parchment paper to lift everything from the pan and place it on a cutting board. Cut 12 squares. Enjoy right away or store in an airtight container in the fridge for about 1 week.

Caramel Apple Shortbread Bars

FOR THE CRUST

3 cups blanched almond flour

½ cup unsalted butter, melted

¼ cup agave nectar, honey, or pure maple syrup

1 teaspoon pure vanilla extract

1 teaspoon salt

FOR THE CARAMEL APPLE FILLING

½ cup unsalted butter

½ cup agave nectar

2 tablespoons coconut sugar

1 teaspoon pure vanilla extract

1 teaspoon ground cinnamon

½ teaspoon salt

¼ teaspoon arrowroot flour

3 Honeycrisp apples, peeled, cored, and small cubed

MAKES 12 BARS
PREP: 15 MINUTES
BAKE: 20 MINUTES

Peanut Butter Marshmallow Cookie Bars

One of the most important things I learned in middle school was that if you combine graham crackers and peanut butter, you get something that tastes a lot like Nutter Butter cookies. These bars are a tribute to not only that priceless preteen knowledge but also my favorite sandwich at the time, peanut butter and marshmallow fluff. I posted this recipe on social media and my literary agent, Leigh, immediately messaged me and said, "Put it in the book!" It seemed like a no-brainer because the recipe was a hands-down hit.

1½ cups natural peanut butter

1 cup coconut sugar

1 teaspoon pure vanilla extract

½ teaspoon salt

2 eggs

9 gluten-free graham crackers (1 pack)

1 cup marshmallow fluff

Flaky salt for sprinkling

MAKES 16 BARS
PREP: 10 MINUTES
BAKE: 20 MINUTES

Preheat the oven to 350°F. Line a 9-inch square pan with parchment paper so that it lines the bottom and drapes over two sides of the pan.

In a large bowl, combine the peanut butter, coconut sugar, vanilla, salt, and eggs. Use an electric mixer on medium-low speed to mix until combined.

Crush the graham crackers. I find it easiest to just keep them in their 9-cracker pack and crush them with your hands. Open the pack and pour them right into the cookie dough. Then add the marshmallow fluff. Use a rubber spatula to gently fold the crackers and marshmallow fluff into the dough. Don't overmix because you want the fluff to ribbon throughout the bars.

Transfer the dough to the prepared pan. Use the rubber spatula to press the dough into the pan in an even layer.

Bake for 20 minutes, until the edges are puffed and the center is just set. Remove the bars from the oven, sprinkle with flaky salt, and allow the bars to come to room temperature. Then transfer to the fridge for 20 minutes to set.

Slide a knife around the sides where the bars touch the pan, then pull the edges of the parchment paper to lift everything from the pan and place it on a cutting board. Cut into 16 squares. Bars can be stored in an airtight container at room temperature for about 3 days or in the fridge for about 2 weeks.

Oatmeal Chocolate Chip Carmelita Bars

The year 2014 was the year of carmelita bars. It went something like this: I found some random recipe on the Internet, became obsessed, and on a near-weekly basis, I'd strap my baby to the front of me, wrestle shoes onto my toddler, assemble the stroller, walk a few blocks to the corner store of our south Philly neighborhood, and buy those little individually wrapped caramels. I'd walk home, spend ages unwrapping them, and proceed to make my new favorite recipe, thus restoring my sanity with every bite. I re-create that original recipe here with my homemade caramels and nutty almond flour.

Preheat the oven to 350°F. Line an 8-inch square pan with parchment paper.

In a medium bowl, whisk together the butter, coconut sugar, and vanilla. Add the almond flour, oats, baking soda, and salt. Use a rubber spatula to fold all the ingredients together until incorporated. Transfer two-thirds of the oat mixture to the prepared pan and use your hands to press it down in an even layer.

Bake for 10 minutes, until the bottom layer is golden brown around the edges. (This is a good time to make the caramel or unwrap the candies.) Remove the base from the oven (but keep the oven on).

Heat the caramel in a small bowl in the microwave (or in a small saucepan over medium-high heat) and whisk until smooth.

Sprinkle the chocolate chips on top of the base layer. Then drizzle the warm caramel over the chocolate chips. Finally, crumble the remaining oat mixture on top of the caramel.

Bake for 15 minutes, until the top is slightly golden and the caramel is bubbly. Remove the bars from the oven and allow them to cool to room temperature. They will be a bit jiggly but will set as they cool.

Chill the bars in the fridge to set until you're ready to cut them into 12 pieces.

½ cup unsalted butter, melted

½ cup coconut sugar

1 teaspoon pure vanilla extract

1 cup blanched almond flour

1 cup gluten-free rolled oats

1 teaspoon baking soda

½ teaspoon salt

1 batch warm caramel (see Salted Caramel Chews, page 144)

½ cup chocolate chips of choice

MAKES 12 BARS
PREP: 10 MINUTES
BAKE: 25 MINUTES

Turtle Brownies

My grandfather lived in a town (Strathmere, New Jersey) that had "turtle crossing" signs all over it. In peak seasons, turtle activity was ranked from high to low so you knew how alert to be. At any moment, you may need to yield and help the turtles on their journey across the road. Turtle candies are named because they kinda sorta look like turtles from the top—the caramel and chocolate shell, the pecan limbs. These brownies look nothing like their reptile namesake, but they hit on all those sweet turtle candy notes.

1 cup coconut sugar

½ cup unsalted butter, melted

1 teaspoon pure vanilla extract

2 eggs

1 cup blanched almond flour

¼ cup cocoa powder

¼ teaspoon salt

1 batch warm caramel (see Salted Caramel Chews, page 144)

1 cup whole pecans

½ cup semisweet chocolate chips

MAKES 16 BROWNIES
PREP: 20 MINUTES
BAKE: 30 MINUTES

Preheat the oven to 350°F. Line a 9-inch square pan with parchment paper.

In a large bowl, whisk together the coconut sugar, butter, vanilla, and eggs until combined. Add the almond flour, cocoa powder, and salt, stirring to combine. Transfer the batter to the prepared pan, spreading it out in an even layer.

Bake for 30 minutes, until the center is set. Remove the brownies from the oven and set aside while you make the caramel.

Gently pour the caramel on the brownies. Top with the pecans. (I like to arrange the pecans in a single layer, but you can definitely sprinkle them on if that's easier for you.) Sprinkle the chocolate chips on top and give the pan a quick shake to nuzzle the chocolate chips between the pecans.

Allow the brownies to cool out on the counter for about 2 hours, until the caramel is set. For a quicker turnaround and a more set caramel topping, chill in the fridge for at least 1 hour. Cut into 16 pieces.

NOTE: *Complete the first step of Salted Caramel Chews to ensure the caramel is warm enough for this recipe. I recommend making the caramel as soon as the brownies come out of the oven.*

Nine and a half times out of ten, I'm picking pecan pie over any other type of pie. I know, I know, I have a whole pie chapter, and I'm going to somehow reconcile this bold claim. But pecan pie is always going to be my first slice at Thanksgiving. The caramel notes, the nutty chunks—my mouth is watering just thinking about it! Now I'm bringing pecan pie out of the holidays and into our everyday lives with these bars.

To make the shortbread, preheat the oven to 350°F. Line a 9-inch square pan with parchment paper.

In a medium bowl, whisk together the butter, agave, and vanilla until combined. Add the almond flour and salt. Whisk again until combined. (It may be easier to use a rubber spatula to incorporate all the ingredients.) Transfer the mixture to the prepared pan and pat it down in an even layer.

Bake for 12 minutes, until the edges are golden brown. Remove the shortbread from the oven and allow it to sit for a few minutes on the range (but keep the oven on). The shortbread can be a bit jiggly, so this will cool it off and firm it up.

While the shortbread bakes, make the topping: Add the butter to a small saucepan over medium-high heat to melt it. Once melted, add the coconut sugar, agave, vanilla, and salt. Whisk vigorously, for about 1 minute, until thickened and incorporated. It may initially look like it's separating but continue to whisk until it comes together. Remove the caramel from the heat and fold in the pecans.

Once the shortbread is firmed up, gently pour the pecan mixture on top. Use a rubber spatula to shimmy the pecans into an even-ish layer. It doesn't have to be perfect because, as it heats in the oven, it will settle into a more even layer.

Bake for 18–20 minutes, until the top is bubbly and the edges are light brown. Remove the bars from the oven and allow them to cool completely. Cut into 16 bars and sprinkle with flaky salt. My husband likes these best chilled, so feel free to pop them in the fridge until you're ready to cut into them.

Salted Caramel Pecan Shortbread Bars

FOR THE SHORTBREAD

½ cup unsalted butter, melted

¼ cup agave nectar, honey, or pure maple syrup

1 teaspoon pure vanilla extract

2½ cups blanched almond flour

½ teaspoon salt

FOR THE CARAMEL PECAN TOPPING

½ cup unsalted butter

½ cup coconut sugar

¼ cup agave nectar, honey, or pure maple syrup

1 teaspoon pure vanilla extract

¼ teaspoon salt

2 cups chopped pecans

Flaky salt for sprinkling

MAKES 16 BARS
PREP: 15 MINUTES
BAKE: 30 MINUTES

Almond Butter Cookie Bars

If you want to switch up your regular blondies or peanut butter cookies, these bars will surely do the trick. The melty chocolate topping and gooey almond butter texture get me every single time.

1½ cups natural almond butter

1 cup coconut sugar

1 teaspoon pure vanilla extract

½ teaspoon baking soda

½ teaspoon salt

2 eggs

½ cup chopped milk chocolate

Flaky salt for sprinkling

MAKES 16 BARS
PREP: 10 MINUTES
BAKE: 20 MINUTES

Preheat the oven to 350°F. Line an 8-inch square pan with parchment paper so that it lines the bottom and drapes over two sides of the pan.

In a large bowl, whisk together the almond butter, coconut sugar, vanilla, baking soda, salt, and eggs until completely combined.

Transfer the batter to the prepared pan and use a rubber spatula to press it into an even layer across the bottom of the pan. Sprinkle the top with the chocolate.

Bake for 20 minutes, until the bars puff up and the edges are set. Remove the bars from the oven and allow them to cool for 15 minutes. They'll deflate a bit as they cool.

Slide a knife around the sides where the bars touch the pan, then pull the edges of the parchment paper to lift everything from the pan and place it on a cutting board. Sprinkle with flaky salt, and cut into 16 bars. Store in an airtight container at room temperature for about 3 days or in the fridge for about 1 week.

Raise your hand if you grew up eating those rectangular chocolate cookie ice cream sandwiches. They are one of my favorite nostalgic treats that I still grab whenever the opportunity arises. The chocolate bookends of these ice cream sandwiches are prepared from a homemade brownie brittle. It boasts rich brownie flavor and the texture of a crisp cookie, creating a sturdy ice cream sandwich that doesn't fall apart in your hands.

The night before you make the the sandwiches, line a 9-inch square pan with parchment paper so that it lines the bottom and drapes over two sides of the pan. Transfer the vanilla ice cream to the prepared pan, spread it out in a smooth layer, and freeze overnight.

Preheat the oven to 350°F. Line a large baking sheet with parchment paper.

In a large bowl, melt the butter in the microwave. (Alternatively, use a double boiler.) Add the coconut sugar, vanilla, and eggs. Whisk until combined. Add the almond flour, cocoa powder, baking powder, and salt. Whisk again until combined. Pour the batter into the prepared baking sheet and spread it into a thin layer across the entire pan.

Bake for 12 minutes, until the center is set. Remove the brownie from the oven and allow it to cool for 20 minutes.

Use a pizza cutter or knife to cut the brownie into 18 rectangles. Use a spatula to break them away from each other and remove them from the pan.

Remove the ice cream from the freezer. Lift the parchment paper up from the square pan to remove the ice cream block and place on a cutting board. Cut it into 10 long rectangles. You will have more ice cream rectangles than you need, but this creates the best shape to fit into the brownie.

Use a spatula to lift an ice cream rectangle and place it on a brownie. Place another on top of the ice cream to sandwich it. Continue until you've used all the brownies.

Enjoy immediately or wrap them individually and freeze them for later.

Brownie Brittle Ice Cream Sandwiches

1 gallon French vanilla ice cream

4 tablespoons unsalted butter

1 cup coconut sugar

1 teaspoon pure vanilla extract

2 eggs

¾ cup blanched almond flour

3 tablespoons cocoa powder

½ teaspoon baking powder

¼ teaspoon salt

MAKES 9 SANDWICHES
PREP: 35 MINUTES
BAKE: 12 MINUTES

Layered S'more Freezer Cake Bars

It took until my twenties before I could roast a marshmallow to a beautiful toasty brown. I was impatient. I roasted too close to the flame. As I grew wiser, I realized how make or break that delicate roasting step is. If you have trouble with the roasting process, or don't have a fire handy, or just want a fun dessert to make for friends, these bars will be a quick favorite.

FOR THE BASE

18 gluten-free graham crackers (2 packs)

2 egg yolks

2 tablespoons agave nectar, honey, or pure maple syrup

1½ cups heavy cream

1 cup semisweet chocolate chips

FOR THE FLUFF TOPPING

2 egg whites

⅓ cup agave nectar, honey, or pure maple syrup

½ cup marshmallow fluff

1 teaspoon pure vanilla extract

MAKES 10 BARS

PREP: 20 MINUTES + 3 HOURS CHILL TIME

To make the base, line a 9-inch bread pan with parchment paper so that it lines the bottom and drapes over two sides of the pan.

Place a single layer of graham crackers across the bottom of the prepared pan. We're going to work in layers, so we'll come back to the rest of the graham crackers later; set them aside.

In a small bowl, whisk the egg yolks for 2 minutes until thick and yellow. Whisk in the agave.

Heat the cream in a small saucepan over medium heat until hot, then turn the heat down to low. Slowly stir at least half of the hot cream into the egg yolk mixture. Work slowly—you don't want to scramble the eggs! Pour everything back into the saucepan and whisk together to combine.

Cook, stirring constantly and making sure the mixture doesn't boil, for about 5 minutes, until it thickens. Stir in the chocolate chips until melted.

Spread some of the chocolate mixture on top of the graham cracker layer. Once they are covered, add another graham cracker layer. Continue this process until all the chocolate is used up, making sure to finish with a chocolate layer.

To make the fluff topping, place the egg whites in a large bowl. Use an electric mixer on high speed to whip them until soft peaks form, about 5 minutes. Set aside.

Place the agave in a small saucepan over medium heat. Whisk constantly until the temperature reaches 160°F.

Begin whipping the egg whites again, slowly drizzling in the hot agave as you mix. Add the marshmallow fluff and vanilla and continue to whip on high until stiff peaks form, about 5 minutes.

Dollop the fluff mixture on top of the final chocolate layer, using a small rubber spatula or the back of a spoon to make swoops and curls in the topping. Cover with aluminum foil and chill in the freezer for at least 3 hours but preferably overnight.

Slide a knife around the edges that touch the pan, then pull up the sides of the parchment paper to lift everything from the pan and place it on a cutting board. Use a sharp knife to cut into 10 bars.

Cannoli Brownie Bites

I only ever remember having cannoli at postbaptism parties. Random, I know. I have thirty some cousins on my Grimes side, so when I was a kid, it seemed there was a baptism every weekend. We'd go back to someone's house, I'd eye the dessert table, and inevitably grab cannoli. The struggle of that tube-shaped shell left little me quite a mess, covered in crumbs and a cloud of powdered sugar. These brownie bites topped with cannoli cream, chocolate bits, and powdered sugar hit all the right notes and leave the struggle behind.

FOR THE TOPPING

15 oz whole milk ricotta

½ cup heavy cream

⅓ cup agave nectar

½ teaspoon pure vanilla extract

½ teaspoon ground cinnamon

FOR THE BROWNIES

6 tablespoons unsalted butter, melted

1 cup coconut sugar

2 eggs

1 cup blanched almond flour

¼ cup cocoa powder

½ teaspoon baking powder

¼ teaspoon salt

¼ cup mini chocolate chips or shaved chocolate

1 tablespoon powdered sugar (optional)

MAKES 12 BITES

PREP: 45 MINUTES
BAKE: 18 MINUTES

To make the topping, place the ricotta in a clean, thin kitchen towel or cheesecloth and squeeze out extra liquid. Set aside.

In a medium bowl, use an electric mixer on high speed to whip the cream until stiff peaks begin to form, 5–7 minutes. Add the agave, vanilla, and cinnamon. This will loosen up the cream, so whip until those peaks turn stiff again. Add the ricotta and fold to incorporate throughout.

Transfer the topping to a piping bag or a large zip-top bag and seal it. Chill in the fridge while you make the brownies.

To make the brownies, preheat the oven to 350°F. Line a 12-cup muffin pan with liners.

In a large bowl, whisk together the butter, coconut sugar, and eggs until combined. Add the almond flour, cocoa powder, baking powder, and salt. Whisk again until combined. Evenly divide the brownie batter among the prepared cups.

Bake for 18–20 minutes, until the tops are puffed up and the centers are set. Remove the brownies from the oven and allow them to cool for 5 minutes, then transfer them to a wire rack to cool completely.

Remove the topping from the fridge. If using a zip-top bag, cut off one corner (about ½ inch). Pipe the topping in a circular motion to frost the tops. Sprinkle with the chocolate chips and sift powdered sugar (if using) on top. Store in an airtight container in the fridge for about 5 days.

Intensely Fudgy Brookies

I could spend hours in Trader Joe's. I love their rotating seasonal items and discovering fun new treats. Something to keep your eye out for in the baked goods section? Brookies have a layer of brownies on the bottom and a layer of chocolate chip cookie on top. It's impossible not to eat them all within 24 hours. My goal here was to achieve that same fudgy, sink-your-teeth-into texture that consumes your mouth in the most intense and delightful way. The oat flour contributes density to the brookies and the chocolate in the brownie base ensures every bite is filled with decadence.

FOR THE BROWNIE BASE

1½ cup semisweet chocolate chips

½ cup coconut sugar

¼ cup agave nectar, honey, or pure maple syrup

2 eggs

1 egg yolk

1 teaspoon pure vanilla extract

½ cup oat flour

¼ cup cocoa powder

½ teaspoon salt

FOR THE COOKIE TOP

½ cup unsalted butter, melted

½ cup coconut sugar

1 egg

1 teaspoon pure vanilla extract

1 cup oat flour

½ teaspoon baking soda

½ teaspoon salt

½ cup semisweet chocolate chips

MAKES 16 BARS
PREP: 15 MINUTES
BAKE: 18 MINUTES

To make the brownie base, preheat the oven to 375°F. Line a 9-inch square pan with parchment paper so that it lines the bottom and drapes over two sides of the pan.

In a large bowl, melt the chocolate chips in the microwave, stirring every 30 seconds until smooth. (Alternatively, use a double boiler.) Add the coconut sugar, agave, eggs, egg yolk, and vanilla. Whisk until smooth. Add the oat flour, cocoa powder, and salt. Whisk again until combined. Transfer the batter to the prepared pan and spread it out in an even layer across the bottom. Set aside.

To make the cookie top, in a separate large bowl, whisk together the butter and coconut sugar. Add the egg and vanilla. Whisk again until combined. Add the oat flour, baking soda, and salt. Whisk again until combined. Fold most of the chocolate chips into the dough, saving some to add on top of the brookies.

Transfer the cookie dough into the pan, spreading it across the top of the brownie batter in an even layer. Sprinkle with the reserved chocolate chips.

Bake for 18–20 minutes, until the center is golden brown and puffs up. I like the center to still be a tad bit jiggly when I remove it from the oven so the top layer retains that gooey-cookie texture.

Allow the brookies to cool to room temperature before you dig into them. To really set them, chill in the fridge for about 1 hour.

Slide a knife around the sides where the brookies touch the pan, then pull the edges of the parchment paper to lift everything from the pan and place it on a cutting board. Cut into 16 squares.

Nutella Crispy Treats

Not me sitting on the couch dipping pretzels straight into a large jar of Nutella. Okay, yes me. Many, many times. I am always looking for new ways to consume Nutella, especially more socially appropriate, less couch-potato ways, and so here we are. My first favorite childhood treat merges with my first favorite adult indulgence: crispy treats plus Nutella pretzels all rolled into one. If nothing else, you'll win some friends at the bake sale.

Line a 13 × 9-inch pan with parchment paper so that it lines the bottom and drapes over two sides of the pan.

Place the butter and the marshmallows in a large pot over medium heat. Stir until both are melted and combined, about 5 minutes.

Remove from the heat and add the chocolate hazelnut spread. Mix to incorporate. Add the cereal and smashed pretzels, mixing again until all the cereal is completely coated with the chocolaty marshmallow. Stir in the remaining 1 cup of marshmallows so they are incorporated and leave fluffy clouds throughout.

Transfer the cereal mixture to the prepared pan. Use a crumbled piece of parchment paper or a rubber spatula to press the mixture in an even layer across the bottom of the pan. If you're feeling fancy, press whole pretzels on top of the treats.

Allow the treats to cool for about 20 minutes, then pull the edges of the parchment paper to lift everything from the pan and place it on a cutting board. Cut into 16 bars. Store in an airtight container at room temperature for about 1 week.

6 tablespoons salted butter

1 (10-oz) bag + 1 cup mini marshmallows (divided)

1 cup chocolate hazelnut spread, such as Nutella

4 cups puffed rice cereal

1 cup smashed pretzels

Whole pretzels for topping (optional)

MAKES 16 LARGE BARS

PREP: 10 MIN + 1 HOUR SET TIME

Cakes & Cupcakes

There is this family story about "going to see the cakes" when I was four years old. It's one of those legendary stories that gets told to new people so they know my true character, my priorities, my heart.

In the late 1980s, my family was out at a local diner grabbing something to eat. I don't remember who was there or where we were, but I do remember walking past the most beautiful cake display when we entered. It was encased in glass, lights enshrining the confections in near-heavenly halo. Shelves of cakes rotated around a center axis, giving each one a moment to shine. My eyes were glued to the display as we passed on our way to the table.

The story goes that I was being a nuisance to other patrons trying to enjoy a quiet meal (a detail I dispute) and in an effort to corral me, my dad asked if I "wanted to go see the cakes." Of course I wanted to see the cakes! To stare at the beautiful, spinning display of all my favorite things? I happily hopped in my dad's arms to be carried to the presentation. As we approached the cakes, my eyes brightened, my heart felt full. But we didn't stop at the cakes. My dad walked straight out the door. The moment I realized I was duped, I began to kick and scream. No! The cakes! I grabbed my little hands onto the doorframe and held on with all my might, getting one last look at the promised sweets.

They say there was restaurant silence. They say there were stares. They say there were little fingernail scratches along the doorway as I was pulled away from that sugary display. But I will never forget the cakes.

Funfetti Birthday Cake

I love that my recipes become a part of your memories. Whenever my recipes end up in your life, be it a simple snack or a grand celebration, I feel honored. This funfetti birthday cake is a great party dessert. You can bake it in round pans, square pans, or even a baking sheet! Mix in your favorite sprinkles.

FOR THE CAKE

½ cup unsalted butter, melted

⅓ cup agave nectar, honey, or pure maple syrup

1 teaspoon pure vanilla extract

3 eggs

1 cup oat flour

2 teaspoons baking powder

½ teaspoon salt

½ cup rainbow sprinkles

FOR THE FROSTING

½ cup heavy cream

1 teaspoon arrowroot flour

1 cup cold unsalted butter, cubed

½ cup agave nectar, honey, or pure maple syrup

2 teaspoons pure vanilla extract

1 teaspoon salt

Food coloring of choice

MAKES 1 CAKE
PREP: 15 MINUTES
BAKE: 20 MINUTES

To make the cake, preheat the oven to 350°F. Line two 6-inch round pans with parchment paper and grease the sides of the pan.

In a medium bowl, whisk together the butter, agave, vanilla, and eggs until combined. Add the oat flour, baking powder, and salt. Whisk again until combined. Add the sprinkles and fold them in until incorporated. Allow the batter to sit for 10 minutes to thicken a bit. Use a rubber spatula to mix the batter once more, then divide it between the prepared pans and spread it out in an even layer.

Bake for 20–23 minutes, until the edges are golden brown and the centers are set. Remove the cakes from the oven and allow them to cool in the pans to room temperature. Slide a knife around the edges of the pans and transfer the cakes to a wire rack to cool completely.

To make the frosting, place the cream and arrowroot flour in a small saucepan over medium heat. Whisk continuously for about 20 seconds, until the cream thickens and pulls away from the sides of the pan as you stir. Remove the pan from the heat and set aside to cool to room temperature.

Place the butter in the bowl of a stand mixer and mix on high speed until light and fluffy, about 2 minutes. While the butter is mixing, drizzle in the agave, vanilla, and salt until combined. Use a rubber spatula to transfer the cream mixture to the bowl along with a few drops of food coloring. Mix on high until combined. If it looks like the mixture is about to curdle—it's okay! Stop the mixer, scrape down the sides with a rubber spatula, and continue to whip on high until fluffy and creamy.

This frosting is best made day of. It hardens in the fridge so if you do make it ahead of time, allow it to come to room temperature before assembling your cake.

To assemble, place one cooled cake on a cake stand or plate and spread some frosting in an even layer on top. Add the second cake on top of the frosting layer. Dollop more frosting on top of the second cake and around the sides. Smooth out until it is spread across the entire cake and sides in an even layer. Cut and serve immediately. For the tastiest experience, enjoy day of.

Chocolate Lava Cakes

At some point in my early twenties, my mom started making lava cakes. The first time I spooned my way into one of those I was shocked! Underbaked? Should we put these back in? As someone who ate most of the brownie batter before it ever hit the oven, I was thrilled to learn that lava cakes were a socially appropriate way to ingest my favorite chocolate indulgence. My mom had a knowing smile. The love I have for warm, gooey chocolate melting and merging into cold vanilla ice cream is unmatched. This is the kind of recipe you won't be able to stop thinking about. Just make sure to grease and liberally dust those ramekins—you have been warned.

Preheat the oven to 400°F. Grease 4 ramekins with butter and then liberally dust them with cocoa powder. The more you dust, the better chances your cakes will turn out and not stick to the ramekins.

In a large bowl, melt the butter and chocolate chips in the microwave, stirring every 30 seconds until smooth. (Alternatively, use a double boiler.) Add the coconut sugar, vanilla, and salt. Whisk again until smooth. Add the eggs and egg yolks. Whisk again until combined. Finally, add the almond flour and whisk until combined. Divide the batter among the prepared ramekins and place them on a small baking sheet.

Bake for 11 minutes, until the tops are set but the cakes are still jiggly when you shake them. Remove the cakes from the oven and allow them to sit for 30 seconds before you turn each one over onto a plate. The longer they sit in the ramekins, the more they'll cook, so, if you want that gooey center, work quickly.

Top with vanilla ice cream and serve with raspberries.

½ cup salted butter + more for greasing ramekins

Cocoa powder for dusting ramekins

1¼ cups semisweet chocolate chips

⅓ cup coconut sugar

1 teaspoon pure vanilla extract

½ teaspoon salt

2 eggs

2 egg yolks

⅔ cup blanched almond flour

Vanilla ice cream for serving

Fresh raspberries for serving

MAKES 4 CAKES
PREP: 15 MINUTES
BAKE: 12 MINUTES

Chocolate Olive Oil Cake

Your cocoa powder will make or break this cake. The chocolate flavor is derived from the cocoa, so starting with a good-quality cocoa that isn't too bitter is the only way to go. I sprinkle powdered sugar on top to finish this cake off and provide some sweetness. If you want to double down on the death-by-chocolate vibes, serve with Hot Fudge Sauce (page 175).

¾ cup extra-virgin olive oil + more for greasing pan

3 eggs

⅔ cup coconut sugar

1½ cups blanched almond flour

½ cup cocoa powder

2 teaspoons baking powder

½ teaspoon salt

Powdered sugar for dusting

MAKES 1 CAKE
PREP: 10 MINUTES
BAKE: 30 MINUTES

Preheat the oven to 325°F. Line a 9-inch round pan with parchment paper. Grease the pan with olive oil.

In a large bowl, whisk together the olive oil, eggs, and coconut sugar. Add the almond flour, cocoa powder, baking powder, and salt. Whisk again until the dry ingredients are incorporated. Pour the batter into the prepared pan and spread it out in an even layer.

Bake for 30–35 minutes, until the top is set and a toothpick comes out clean. Remove the cake from the oven and and allow it to cool in the pan for about 10 minutes.

Use a butter knife to slide around the edges of the cake. Turn the cake over onto a plate and tap on the bottom to release it from the pan. Place another plate on the bottom of the cake and flip it again so the top is facing up.

Allow the cake to cool to room temperature, then sprinkle the top with powdered sugar and cut into 12 slices.

This recipe is a lot like a brownie cake, and I'm here for it. I love adding some espresso powder to rich, chocolate desserts to give them deeper flavor.

Preheat the oven to 350°F. Line a 9-inch springform pan with parchment paper.

In a large bowl, melt the chocolate chips and butter in the microwave, stirring every 30 seconds until smooth. (Alternatively, use a double boiler.) Whisk in the coconut sugar, vanilla, eggs, and egg yolks until combined and smooth. Add the almond flour, espresso powder, and salt. Whisk again until combined. Transfer the batter to the prepared pan and spread it out in an even layer.

Bake for 30 minutes, until the center is set and a toothpick comes out clean. Remove the cake from the oven and allow it to cool for about 10 minutes before releasing the pan and removing the cake.

Sift powdered sugar on top and cut into 16 to 18 slices.

Chocolate Espresso Cake

1 cup semisweet chocolate chips

½ cup unsalted butter

⅓ cup coconut sugar

1 teaspoon pure vanilla extract

2 eggs

2 egg yolks

1 cup blanched almond flour

2 tablespoons instant espresso powder

½ teaspoon salt

Powdered sugar or cocoa powder for dusting

MAKES 1 CAKE
PREP: 15 MINUTES
BAKE: 30 MINUTES

Chocolate Chunk Banana Cake

Bananas go one of two ways in my house: The bunch is consumed within a day, or they sit on the counter until they turn all spotty, begging to be used. Those spotty bananas always get me a bit excited because that means I can bake something sweet and cakey and probably loaded with chocolate. While banana bread is always my go-to, when I want my baked treat to last a little longer or have somewhere to take it, banana cake is great for slicing and sharing! Drizzle it with chocolate sauce, take a bite, and drizzle some more.

4 very ripe bananas, mashed
(about 2 cups mashed)

4 eggs

½ cup natural peanut butter

⅓ cup agave nectar, honey,
or pure maple syrup

⅓ cup coconut sugar

3 cups blanched almond flour

3 teaspoons baking powder

½ teaspoon salt

1½ cups dark chocolate chunks
(divided)

½ cup unsweetened coconut cream

MAKES 1 CAKE

PREP: 15 MINUTES
BAKE: 50 MINUTES

Preheat the oven to 350°F. Generously grease a Bundt pan or a 10-inch round pan.

In a large bowl, whisk together the mashed bananas, eggs, peanut butter, agave, and coconut sugar until combined. Add the almond flour, baking powder, and salt. Whisk again until combined. Fold in 1 cup of chocolate chunks. Transfer the batter to the prepared pan and spread it out in an even layer.

Bake for 50–55 minutes, until the cake is firm and bounces back when you press on the top. If the top is getting too brown, cover with aluminum foil and continue baking. Remove the cake from the oven and allow it to cool in the pan for about 15 minutes. Place the plate of a cake stand on top of the pan and turn it over to release the cake. If needed, give the pan a few encouraging taps.

While the cake is baking, in a small saucepan over medium heat, whisk together the remaining ½ cup of chocolate chunks and the coconut cream until melted and smooth, about 5 minutes.

Drizzle the chocolate icing on the cake and cut into slices.

A trifle is an English dessert that I never knew existed until it showed up one day on my social media feed flaunting its beautiful layers. They were so gorgeous, and I loved the concept of a make-ahead treat that could give me some artistic wiggle room.

To make the cake, preheat the oven to 350°F. Line a 13 × 9-inch pan with parchment paper so that it lines the bottom and drapes over two sides of the pan.

In a large bowl, whisk together the eggs, butter, agave, peanut butter, and vanilla until combined. Add the almond flour, baking powder, and salt. Whisk again until combined. Transfer the batter to the prepared pan, using a rubber spatula to spread it out in an even layer.

Bake for 20 minutes, until the edges are golden brown and the center is set. Remove the cake from the oven and allow it to cool completely in the pan before assembling the trifle—you don't want the whip to melt!

To make the peanut butter whip, when you're ready to assemble the trifle, place the cream, peanut butter, and agave in the bowl of a stand mixer. Whip on high speed until it fluffs up and stiff peaks form.

Slide a knife around the sides where the cake touches the pan, then pull the edges of the parchment paper to lift the cake from the pan and place it on a cutting board. Cut into 1 × ½-inch pieces.

Line the cake pieces around the inside circumference of a trifle dish. I take care to line the outside perfectly because that's what shows on the outside. Fill the inside with more cake pieces, but you don't have to be as particular with them. Add a layer of peanut butter cups around the perimeter, touching the glass, but don't fill the inside. Then add a few dollops of the whip and spread it out in an even layer. Continue this process with another layer of cake, candy, and whip until you run out.

Scoop into individual bowls.

Peanut Butter Dream Trifle

FOR THE CAKE

3 eggs

½ cup unsalted butter, softened

½ cup agave nectar, honey, or pure maple syrup

¼ cup natural peanut butter

1 teaspoon pure vanilla extract

2 cups blanched almond flour

1 teaspoon baking powder

½ teaspoon salt

FOR THE PEANUT BUTTER WHIP

2 cups heavy cream

¼ cup natural peanut butter

¼ cup agave nectar, honey, or pure maple syrup

30+ mini peanut butter cups, halved or roughly chopped

SERVES 8
PREP: 20 MINUTES
BAKE: 20 MINUTES

Coffee Walnut Chocolate Chip Cake

Every Christmas, my mom would bake homemade cakes and breads for our neighbors. My favorite loaf was—and is—her coffee walnut chocolate chip bread. My brother and I oversaw delivery with a big smile and a "Merry Christmas!" One year, feeling the holiday spirit, our neighbor brought out a cookie tray and let us take our pick. I locked eyes with a gingerbread man three times bigger than any other cookie on the tray. I snatched him up and skipped down the street back home. Only after I powered through my second grainy, tooth-cracking bite did I hear the urgent footsteps behind us. Turns out the giant gingerbread man was no cookie at all but rather a ceramic tray decoration. No hard feelings here, I said, and hoped the holiday loaf was enjoyed.

3 eggs

½ cup unsalted butter, melted

⅓ cup agave nectar, honey, or pure maple syrup

2 tablespoons instant espresso powder

1 teaspoon pure vanilla extract

1 cup oat flour

2 teaspoons baking powder

½ teaspoon salt

½ cup mini chocolate chips

½ cup chopped walnuts

MAKES 1 CAKE

PREP: 10 MINUTES
BAKE: 25 MINUTES

Preheat the oven to 350°F. Line a 9-inch square pan with parchment paper.

In a large bowl, whisk together the eggs, butter, agave, espresso powder, and vanilla until combined. Add the oat flour, baking powder, and salt. Whisk again until combined. Using a rubber spatula, fold in the chocolate chips and walnuts and allow to sit for about 5 minutes. (Oat flour thickens a bit as it sits.) Transfer the batter to the prepared pan and spread it out in an even layer.

Bake for 25–27 minutes, until the edges are golden brown, popped bubbles appear on the top, and the center is set when you give the pan a jiggle. Remove the cake from the oven and allow it to cool completely in the pan. Remove the cake from the pan and cut it into 16 squares.

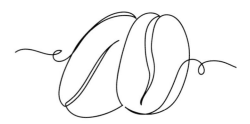

I heard a certain actor sends coconut cake to all his costars that he enjoyed working with. It's a sign of pride to have received a cake from this man. Since I probably will never star in an action movie alongside him to win him over with my charm, I'll just make my own. But instead of coconut cake, we're baking cupcakes so you, too, can share them with all your favorite people. They are light and fluffy, like biting into a delicious coconut cloud.

To make the cupcakes, preheat the oven to 350°F. Line a 12-cup muffin pan with liners.

Place the shredded coconut in a small frying pan over medium-low heat. Stir it frequently for about 5 minutes, until the coconut is light, toasty brown, and fragrant. Transfer to a small bowl and set aside.

In a medium bowl, whisk together the butter, agave, vanilla, and eggs until combined. Add the oat flour, baking powder, and salt. Whisk again until combined. Use a rubber spatula to fold in most of the toasted coconut, saving about 1 tablespoon to decorate the finished cupcakes. Allow the batter to sit for 3–5 minutes to thicken. Evenly divide the batter among the prepared cups.

Bake for 15–17 minutes, until the tops puff up and bounce back when you touch them. Remove the cupcakes from the oven. Turn the cupcakes out onto a wire rack and allow them to cool completely.

To make the cloud fluff, place the egg whites and agave in a small saucepan over medium heat. Whisk constantly until the temperature reaches 160°F. Transfer to a large bowl and add the marshmallow fluff and coconut extract.

Use an electric mixer on high speed to whip the mixture until stiff peaks form. Transfer the fluff to a piping bag and create fluffy swirled clouds on top of the cooled cupcakes. Alternatively, use a small spatula to spread it on the tops.

Sprinkle the tops with the remaining toasted coconut.

Toasted Coconut Cupcakes

FOR THE CUPCAKES

½ cup unsweetened shredded coconut

½ cup unsalted butter, melted

⅓ cup agave nectar, honey, or pure maple syrup

1 teaspoon pure vanilla extract

3 eggs

¾ cup oat flour

2 teaspoons baking powder

½ teaspoon salt

FOR THE CLOUD FLUFF

2 egg whites

⅓ cup agave nectar

¼ cup marshmallow fluff

½ teaspoon coconut extract

MAKES 12 CUPCAKES

PREP: 15 MINUTES
BAKE: 15 MINUTES

Lemon Curd Poke Cake

If you love the involuntary puckering of tangy treats—you know the ones that are sour yet slightly sweet and entice you to return bite after bite, entangling you in some sort of reflexive relationship—you're about to be delighted. Lemon curd poke cake will have your mouth in twists. From its moist crumb to its silky citrus curd, this cake leaves your mouth watering and your taste buds pining for more.

FOR THE CAKE

2 lemons

½ cup unsalted butter, melted (see note)

¾ cup coconut sugar

3 eggs

1½ cups blanched almond flour

½ cup oat flour

2 teaspoons baking powder

½ teaspoon salt

FOR THE LEMON CURD

4 tablespoons unsalted butter, softened

½ cup agave nectar, honey, or pure maple syrup

4 egg yolks

2 eggs

1 teaspoon grated lemon zest

½ cup fresh lemon juice

MAKES 1 CAKE

PREP: 15 MINUTES + 2+ HOURS CHILL TIME

BAKE: 20 MINUTES

To make the cake, preheat the oven to 350°F. Line a 9-inch square pan with parchment paper.

Zest the lemons over a large bowl, then halve and juice them into a measuring cup (you should have about ¼ cup of juice). Pour the juice through a strainer into the bowl with the zest.

Add the butter, coconut sugar, and eggs to the bowl. Whisk until combined. Add the almond flour, oat flour, baking powder, and salt. Whisk again until combined. Transfer the batter to the prepared pan and spread it out in an even layer.

Bake for 20–25 minutes, until the top is golden brown and the center is set. Remove the cake from the oven and allow it to cool completely in the pan.

To make the lemon curd, in a medium bowl, whisk together the butter and agave until combined. Add the egg yolks, eggs, and lemon zest and juice. Whisk again until combined. Transfer the curd mixture to a small saucepan over medium heat. Whisk constantly for about 5 minutes, until the curd thickens.

Use the back of a wooden spoon to poke holes into the top of the cooled cake. Pour the curd on top of the cake, spreading it out in an even layer.

Chill the cake in the fridge for 2+ hours, until the lemon curd is set. This is a great cake to prep ahead because the curd really comes together and sets in the fridge. Alternatively, you can make the curd ahead to spread on top of a freshly baked and cooled cake. Cut into 16 squares.

NOTE: *For an olive oil–cake variation, substitute your favorite olive oil for the butter used in the batter.*

Take me to the Keys, please! These cupcakes are made with a zesty Key lime cake base and topped with a tangy lime juice glaze that will transport you to a tropical beach with every bite. The lime is balanced with the soft, fluffy, sweet cake. I love the elegance of the glaze, but feel free to top these little cakes with a lime wedge, mint leaf, or even a dollop of whipped cream. You don't need to be sipping a rum runner on the beach to enjoy these cupcakes (but it does sound nice).

To make the cupcakes, preheat the oven to 350°F. Line a 12-cup muffin pan with liners.

In a large bowl, whisk together the eggs, butter, agave, and lime juice until combined. Add the almond flour, oat flour, baking powder, and salt. Whisk again until combined. Evenly divide the batter among the prepared cups. I like using an ice cream scoop to help me evenly distribute all the batter.

Bake for 20 minutes, until the tops are puffed up and set. Remove the cupcakes from the oven and allow them to cool in the pan for 20 minutes before glazing.

To make the glaze, in a small bowl, whisk together the powdered sugar and lime juice. Dip the top of each cupcake into the glaze, allow the excess to drip off, and place them on a wire rack or plate. Garnish with lime zest.

Key Lime Cupcakes

FOR THE CUPCAKES

3 eggs

½ cup unsalted butter, melted

½ cup agave nectar, honey, or pure maple syrup

⅓ cup Key lime juice

1½ cups blanched almond flour

½ cup oat flour

2 teaspoons baking powder

½ teaspoon salt

FOR THE GLAZE

1 cup powdered sugar

1 tablespoon key lime juice

Grated lime zest for garnish

MAKES 12 CUPCAKES
PREP: 15 MINUTES
BAKE: 20 MINUTES

Cookie Butter Cake with Sweet Whipped Butter

After I made cookie butter with graham crackers, I willed myself to stop eating the entire batch (the self-control!) because I wanted to take it one step further. I tried swirling the cookie butter into brownies for fudgy blondies. Fail after fail, I realized I needed to follow the clues the cookie butter was giving me. Soft, delicate, fluffy. Cake it is! This slightly sweet cake is perfect for slathering with homemade whipped butter and nibbling with your morning tea. Be the cake you were always meant to be.

1 batch Cookie Butter (page 141)

2 eggs

½ teaspoon baking soda

1 cup unsalted butter, softened

1 tablespoon heavy cream

3 tablespoons coconut sugar

1 teaspoon flaky salt

MAKES 1 CAKE
PREP: 10 MINUTES
BAKE: 20 MINUTES

Preheat the oven to 350°F. Line an 8-inch square pan with parchment paper so that it lines the bottom and drapes over two sides of the pan.

In a large bowl, whisk together the cookie butter, eggs, and baking soda until combined. Transfer the batter to the prepared pan and spread it out in an even layer.

Bake for 20 minutes, until the top is fluffy and the center of the cake bounces back when you gently press it. Remove the cake from the oven and allow it to cool in the pan for about 10 minutes.

While the cake is baking, place the butter and cream in a medium bowl and use an electric mixer on high speed to whip it for 1 minute, until light and fluffy. Add the coconut sugar and flaky salt. Whip again until combined. Transfer to a serving dish with a butter knife.

Slide a knife around the sides where the cake touches the pan, then pull the parchment paper to lift the cake from the pan and place it on a cutting board. Cut it into 16 squares and serve with the whipped butter.

I love butter cake (okay, maybe I love anything leading with butter). But I particularly love butter cake because it has a rich, tender texture that can be dressed up with toppings like frostings, fruit compotes, and saucy drizzles, or it can be enjoyed in its beautiful simplicity.

Preheat the oven to 350°F. Line an 8-inch springform pan with parchment paper.

In a large bowl, use an electric mixer on high speed to cream together the egg yolks, egg, cream cheese, butter, agave, and vanilla until light and fluffy. Add the almond flour and salt and mix again until combined. Transfer the batter to the prepared pan and spread it out in an even layer.

Bake for 30–35 minutes, until the edges are golden brown and the center is set. Remove the cake from the oven and allow it to cool in the pan for 10 minutes before releasing the springform pan and cutting the cake into 8 slices.

Butter Cake

2 egg yolks

1 egg

2 oz cream cheese, at room temperature

⅓ cup unsalted butter, melted

¼ cup agave nectar, honey, or pure maple syrup

1½ teaspoons vanilla bean paste

1 cup blanched almond flour

½ teaspoon salt

MAKES 1 CAKE
PREP: 10 MINUTES
BAKE: 30 MINUTES

Mint-Chocolate Chip Cupcakes

If you're a big fan of mint chocolate flavors, you'll love these adorable cupcakes! The soft, minty cakes are stuffed with chocolate chips and topped with a classic chocolate frosting that's been given a minty makeover. Make these your own by adorning them with mint leaves or crushed candies. Serve as a festive holiday treat or a refreshing dessert on a hot summer day.

FOR THE FROSTING

12 oz semisweet chocolate chips

1 cup heavy cream or unsweetened coconut cream

2 tablespoons agave nectar, honey, or pure maple syrup

1 teaspoon mint extract

½ teaspoon salt

FOR THE CUPCAKES

3 eggs

½ cup unsalted butter, melted

½ cup agave nectar

2½ cups blanched almond flour

¼ cup oat flour

2 teaspoons baking powder

½ teaspoon salt

5 drops green food coloring, or as needed

¾ cup mini chocolate chips

MAKES 12 CUPCAKES

PREP: 1 HOUR +
2 HOURS CHILL TIME
BAKE: 25 MINUTES

To make the frosting, place the chocolate chips, cream, and agave in a medium saucepan over medium heat. Warm, whisking occasionally, for about 5 minutes, until heated through and the chocolate is melted and incorporated. (Alternatively, you could do this in a microwave, stirring every 30 seconds until the chocolate is melted.) Add the mint extract and salt. Whisk again until combined. Transfer the frosting to a large bowl and chill in the fridge for 2 hours.

To make the cupcakes, preheat the oven to 350°F. Line a 12-cup muffin pan with liners.

In a large bowl, whisk together the eggs, butter, and agave until combined. Add the almond flour, oat flour, baking powder, and salt. Whisk again until combined. Add the food coloring, whisking every few drops to make sure you don't make the batter too dark green. (Mine took about 5 drops to get the perfect minty color, but yours may take more or less.) Add the chocolate chips and fold them into the batter until incorporated. Evenly divide the batter among the prepared cups.

Bake for 25 minutes, until the tops puff up and the edges are golden brown. Remove the cupcakes from the oven and allow them to cool completely before frosting.

When you're ready to frost the cupcakes, remove the frosting from the fridge and allow it to sit at room temperature for about 10 minutes. Use an electric mixer on medium-high speed to whip the frosting until it is soft and fluffy. Transfer to a piping bag and swirl onto the tops of the cupcakes.

Store in an airtight container at room temperature for about 3 days or in the fridge for about 1 week.

For our birthdays in elementary school, my mom would make enough cupcakes to pass out for the class. She'd line them up perfectly in a cardboard clothing box, tie it with baker's twine, and send me off to the bus stop. It's amazing those cupcakes, year after year, made their way to school intact. No matter the occasion, cupcakes are always a crowd-pleaser, for kids and adults alike. Here, the rich, moist chocolate cake is paired with a fudgy frosting. Enjoy them as is or top with sprinkles, chopped nuts, or candy pieces. The frosting needs to chill for 2 hours, so allow enough time to make it ahead.

To make the frosting, place the chocolate chips, cream, agave, and salt in a medium saucepan over medium heat. Warm, whisking occasionally, for about 5 minutes, until heated through and the chocolate is melted and incorporated. (Alternatively, you could do this in a microwave, stirring every 30 seconds until the chocolate is melted.) Whisk again until combined. Transfer the frosting to a large bowl and chill in the fridge for 2 hours.

To make the cupcakes, preheat the oven to 350°F. Line a 12-cup muffin pan with liners.

In a large bowl, whisk together the eggs, butter, agave, and vanilla until combined. Add the oat flour, cocoa powder, baking powder, and salt. Whisk again until combined. Add the chocolate chips and fold into the batter until incorporated. Evenly divide the batter among the prepared cups. They don't rise too much so you can fill them about three-fourths full.

Bake for 20 minutes, until the tops puff a bit (they won't dome too much) and a toothpick comes out clean. Remove the cupcakes from the oven and allow them to cool completely before frosting.

When you're ready to frost the cupcakes, remove the frosting from the fridge and allow it to sit at room temperature for about 10 minutes. Use an electric mixer on medium-high speed to whip the frosting until soft and fluffy, about 5 minutes. Transfer to a piping bag and swirl onto the tops of the cupcakes. Sprinkle some chocolate chips on top.

Chocolate Cupcakes with Chocolate Frosting

FOR THE FROSTING

12 oz semisweet chocolate chips

1 cup heavy cream or unsweetened coconut cream

2 tablespoons agave nectar, honey, or pure maple syrup

½ teaspoon salt

FOR THE CUPCAKES

2 eggs

½ cup unsalted butter, softened

⅓ cup agave nectar, honey, or pure maple syrup

1 teaspoon pure vanilla extract

¾ cup oat flour

¼ cup cocoa powder

2 teaspoons baking powder

½ teaspoon salt

½ cup mini chocolate chips + more for sprinkling

MAKES 12 CUPCAKES

PREP: 30 MINUTES + 2 HOURS CHILL TIME

BAKE: 20 MINUTES

Peanut Butter and Chocolate Donuts

Once I got a donut pan and realized I could easily bake donuts at home, my weekend donut habit became wildly more regular. These cakelike treats are made with peanut butter and have a tender, fluffy texture. Once cooled, they're dipped in a cocoa mixture that turns into a chocolate shell. I love to drizzle them with some peanut butter to hit home that chocolate–peanut butter combo we all love, but chopped nuts or chocolate sprinkles are also delicious.

FOR THE DONUTS

4 tablespoons unsalted butter, softened

¼ cup agave nectar, honey, or pure maple syrup

2 tablespoons natural peanut butter

1 teaspoon pure vanilla extract

2 eggs

1 cup blanched almond flour

1 teaspoon baking powder

½ teaspoon salt

FOR THE CHOCOLATE ICING

¼ cup refined coconut oil, melted

1 tablespoon cocoa powder

1 tablespoon agave nectar

FOR THE PEANUT BUTTER DRIZZLE

2 tablespoons natural peanut butter

1 tablespoon refined coconut oil, melted

MAKES 6 DONUTS
PREP: 15 MINUTES
BAKE: 10 MINUTES

To make the donuts, preheat the oven to 350°F. Grease a metal donut pan with butter or your favorite cooking spray. Or, skip the whole greasing thing and use a silicone pan. (I love silicone pans because the donuts slip right out in one piece.)

In a large bowl, whisk together the butter, agave, peanut butter, vanilla, and eggs until combined. Add the almond flour, baking powder, and salt. Whisk again until combined. Transfer the batter to a zip-top bag and cut off one corner (about ¾ inch). Evenly squeeze the batter out around the circles of the prepared pan.

Bake for 10–12 minutes, until the donuts are golden brown. Remove the donuts from the oven and allow them to cool in the pan for 10 minutes. Slide a butter knife around the edges, gently lift the donuts from the pan, and transfer them to a wire rack to cool completely.

To make the chocolate icing, in a small bowl, warm the coconut oil in the microwave for about 1 minute. Whisk in the cocoa powder and agave until smooth. Dip the tops of the donuts into the chocolate icing and place them back to a wire rack.

To make the peanut butter drizzle, in a separate small bowl, microwave the peanut butter for 30 seconds to 1 minute. Stir in the coconut oil and continue to stir until the peanut butter is completely melted. Drizzle on top of the donuts.

These donuts are delicious day of and best stored in an airtight container at room temperature for about 3 days. They will keep for about 1 week in the fridge in an airtight container.

Orange Chia Mini Bundts

One semester, lemon poppy seed muffins were a daily habit for my 9 a.m. college class. I'd pop by a campus café and grab a coffee and muffin to go. I adored the bright, tart lemon with the seedy bits I could continue to crunch on between mouthfuls. For a new take on the iconic muffin, these mini bundts use different citrus and seeds, giving you that same tang and texture.

2 eggs

¼ cup fresh orange juice, strained

¼ cup agave nectar, honey, or pure maple syrup

2 tablespoons vegetable oil

1 tablespoon grated orange zest

1 cup blanched almond flour

2 tablespoons oat flour

1 tablespoon chia seeds or poppy seeds

1 teaspoon baking powder

½ teaspoon salt

MAKES 12
PREP: 10 MINUTES
BAKE: 18 MINUTES

Preheat the oven to 350°F. Grease a 12-cup mini bundt pan (or two 6-cup mini bundt pans). (I prefer silicone bundt pans, which don't require greasing and make it easy to remove the cakes.) If you're using silicone pans, place them on a baking sheet to keep them flat in the oven.

In a medium bowl, whisk together the eggs, orange juice, agave, oil, and orange zest until combined. Add the almond flour, oat flour, chia seeds, baking powder, and salt. Whisk again until combined. Evenly divide the batter among the prepared bundt cavities and give the pan a little jiggle to settle the batter into an even layer. They don't rise too much so you can fill them about three-fourths full. Alternatively, transfer the batter to a large zip-top bag and cut off one corner (about ¾ inch), then pipe the batter into the pan cavities.

Bake for 18–20 minutes, until the tops are set when you touch them. Remove the cakes from the oven and allow them to cool in the pan for about 10 minutes before turning them out onto a wire rack or serving plate.

There was a period of my life when my mom would buy a six-pack of shortcakes for us to top with whipped cream and fresh strawberries. The tradition was light and summery and made me appreciate the delicate treat. But why stop with strawberries? Top these homemade shortcakes with whatever seasonal fruit you like—from figs to peaches to roasted grapes.

To make the shortcakes, preheat the oven to 350°F. Grease a 12-cup mini bundt pan (or two 6-cup mini bundt pans) as needed. (I prefer silicone Bundt pans, which don't require greasing and make it easy to remove the cakes.)

In a large bowl, whisk together the eggs, butter, agave, milk, and vanilla until combined. Add the almond flour, oat flour, baking powder, and salt. Whisk again until combined. Transfer the batter to a piping bag or a large zip-top bag and cut off one corner (about ¾ inch). Squeeze into the prepared bundt cavities. If you're using a silicone pan, place it on a baking sheet to keep it flat in the oven.

Bake for 25–27 minutes, until the tops are golden brown and set when you touch them. Remove the cakes from the oven and allow them to cool in the pan for about 15 minutes before turning them out onto a wire rack.

To make the whipped cream, place the cream, agave, and vanilla in the bowl of a stand mixer. Whip on high speed until it fluffs up and stiff peaks form.

Dollop the whipped cream into the center of each cake and finish them off with the strawberries.

Strawberry Shortcakes

FOR THE SHORTCAKES

3 eggs

½ cup unsalted butter, softened

½ cup agave nectar, honey, or pure maple syrup

⅓ cup whole milk

1½ teaspoons pure vanilla extract

1½ cups blanched almond flour

½ cup oat flour

2 teaspoons baking powder

½ teaspoon salt

FOR THE WHIPPED CREAM

1 cup heavy cream

2 tablespoons agave nectar, honey, or pure maple syrup

1 teaspoon pure vanilla extract

Fresh strawberries, quartered

MAKES 12 SHORTCAKES
PREP: 15 MINUTES
BAKE: 25 MINUTES

When we lived in California, Sidecar Doughnuts had a line out the door. It is known for fresh, artful donuts and my favorite was cinnamon crumb, but my son Caleb loved huckleberry. The gorgeous glaze always caught my eye, standing bright and fruity next to its peers. After we moved back East, I decided to make Caleb my own version of that huckleberry donut—a vanilla base with a simple jammy glaze. Fresh huckleberries can be hard to come by, so I opted for jam that you can find online. Jams can vary in their sugar content, so taste test as you go to get the sweetness level you like.

To make the donuts, preheat the oven to 350°F. Grease a metal donut pan with butter or your favorite cooking spray. Or, skip the whole greasing thing and use a silicone pan. (I love silicone pans because the donuts slip right out in one piece.)

In a large bowl, whisk together the eggs, butter, agave, and vanilla until combined. Add the almond flour, oat flour, baking powder, and salt. Whisk again until combined. Transfer the batter in a zip-top bag and cut off one corner (about ¾ inch). Evenly squeeze the batter out around the circles of the prepared pan. If using a silicone pan, place it on a baking sheet. You won't need a baking sheet under a metal pan.

Bake for 15–18 minutes, until the tops are set and spring back when you touch them. Remove the donuts from the oven and allow them to cool for 10 minutes before transferring to a wire rack to cool completely.

To make the huckleberry glaze, in a small bowl, vigorously whisk the jam, powdered sugar, and oil. If needed, heat it for about 20 seconds in the microwave to make it thin and drippy. Give it a little taste to make sure it's sweet enough.

Dip the tops of the donuts into the glaze. Place them back onto the wire rack or serve immediately.

Huckleberry Donuts

FOR THE DONUTS

2 eggs

4 tablespoons unsalted butter, melted

¼ cup agave nectar, honey, or pure maple syrup

1 teaspoon pure vanilla extract

1 cup blanched almond flour

2 tablespoons oat flour

1 teaspoon baking powder

½ teaspoon salt

FOR THE HUCKLEBERRY GLAZE

3 tablespoons huckleberry jam

3 tablespoons powdered sugar, plus more as needed

1 tablespoon refined coconut oil, melted

MAKES 6 DONUTS
PREP: 10 MINUTES
BAKE: 15 MINUTES

Apple Cider Mini Bundts

Springdale Farm Market, a cute little market close to where I grew up, made a big impression on me. I picked pumpkins and had a birthday party hayride there. Aside from the adorable kittens they had one year in the '90s, the apple cider donuts were my favorite item. At the market, my mom and I would buy a bag of freshly baked donuts coated in cinnamon sugar. I think about those often and about that orange-and-white striped kitten I fell in love with. These mini bundts are a love letter to both—may they bring you all the warm fuzzy memories they brought me.

FOR THE CAKES

½ cup unsalted butter, softened

½ cup agave nectar, honey, or pure maple syrup

⅓ cup apple cider

3 eggs

1½ cups blanched almond flour

½ cup oat flour

2 teaspoons ground cinnamon

2 teaspoons baking powder

½ teaspoon salt

FOR THE TOPPING

1 tablespoon granulated sugar

1 teaspoon ground cinnamon

MAKES 12 MINI BUNDTS
PREP: 10 MINUTES
BAKE: 25 MINUTES

To make the cakes, preheat the oven to 350°F. Grease a 12-cup mini bundt pan (or two 6-cup mini bundt pans) as needed. (I prefer silicone bundt pans, which don't require greasing and make it easy to remove the cakes.)

In a large bowl, vigorously whisk together the butter and agave until combined. Add the cider and eggs. Whisk again until combined. Add the almond flour, oat flour, cinnamon, baking powder, and salt. Whisk again until combined. Transfer the batter to a piping bag or a large zip-top bag and cut off one corner (about ¾ inch). Squeeze in a circular motion into the prepared bundt cavities. If you're using a silicone pan, place it on a baking sheet to keep it flat in the oven.

Bake for 25–27 minutes, until the tops are golden brown and set when you touch them. Remove the cakes from the oven and allow them to cool in the pan for about 15 minutes before turning them out onto a wire rack.

To make the topping, in a small bowl, stir together the granulated sugar and cinnamon. Sprinkle the cakes with the cinnamon sugar.

There is something so delicate and charming about this simple cake. The flavor is gentle with small, fruity bites floating throughout. It's delicious unadorned but you can embellish it with fresh fruit, whipped cream, or ice cream.

Preheat the oven to 350°F. Grease a bundt pan.

In a medium bowl, whisk together the eggs, jam, agave, and vanilla until combined. Add the almond flour, oat flour, baking powder, and salt. Whisk again until smooth. Add the peaches and fold to incorporate. Transfer to the prepared pan and spread it out in an even layer.

Bake for 22–25 minutes, until the top is golden brown and a toothpick comes out clean. Remove the cake from the oven and allow it to cool in the pan for at least 15 minutes.

Place a plate on the top of the pan and turn it over to release it from the pan.

Dust with powdered sugar (if using) and cut into slices.

Stone Fruit Bundt Cake

2 eggs

⅓ cup peach or apricot jam

¼ cup agave nectar, honey, or pure maple syrup

1 teaspoon pure vanilla extract

1 cup blanched almond flour

2 tablespoons oat flour

2 teaspoons baking powder

½ teaspoon salt

½ cup diced peaches (I used jarred peaches in grape juice concentrate, drained and patted dry)

Powdered sugar for dusting (optional)

MAKES 1 CAKE
PREP: 10 MINUTES
BAKE: 22 MINUTES

Blackberry Lemon Crumb Cake

If you love the tartness of fresh blackberries and zesty lemon everything, you will adore this soft and buttery crumb cake. Studded with juicy blackberries and bright lemon flavor, this cake is perfect for serving at brunch. The crumbly, tender texture makes for a light and fresh counterpoint to any rich, decadent dessert.

FOR THE BATTER

6 tablespoons unsalted butter, melted

Zest and juice of 2 lemons (about ½ cup juice)

½ cup coconut sugar

3 eggs

1½ cups blanched almond flour

2 teaspoons baking powder

½ teaspoon salt

FOR THE TOPPING

½ cup fresh blackberries

2 tablespoons salted butter, melted

1 tablespoon agave nectar, honey, or pure maple syrup

¼ cup gluten-free rolled oats

2 tablespoons turbinado sugar

MAKES 1 CAKE
PREP: 15 MINUTES
BAKE: 35 MINUTES

To make the batter, preheat the oven to 350°F. Line a 9-inch square pan with parchment paper.

In a large bowl, whisk together the butter, lemon zest and juice, coconut sugar, and eggs until combined. Add the almond flour, baking powder, and salt. Whisk again until combined. Transfer the batter to the prepared pan, spreading it into the corners. Set aside.

To make the topping, place the blackberries, butter, and agave in a small saucepan over medium heat. Cook, roughly breaking down the blackberries, for about 5 minutes, then remove the pan from the heat. Stir in the oats.

Add the blackberry-oat mixture to the top of the batter, using a rubber spatula or knife to swirl it into the top. Sprinkle the top with the turbinado sugar.

Bake for 35–40 minutes, until the edges are golden brown and the center is set. Remove the cake from the oven and allow it to cool in the pan for at least 15 minutes before removing it from the pan and cutting it into 16 squares.

I love desserts that are served in individual cups. There's something super elegant about placing small ramekins in front of each guest instead of leaning over everyone to plop a slice of cake on their plate. These cappuccino cakes are made with espresso powder, which contributes a rich and velvety flavor that balances beautifully with the cake. If you want to push the indulgence, add a scoop of ice cream and a drizzle of caramel.

Ramekin Cappuccino Cakes

Preheat the oven to 350°F.

In a large bowl, whisk together the coconut sugar, cream, oil, and egg until combined. Add the almond flour, espresso powder, baking soda, and salt. Whisk again until combined. Evenly divide the batter among 4 ramekins and place on a baking sheet.

Bake for 20 minutes, until the centers are flat and set. As these bake, the centers dip and are the last to rise. The tops will be flat and cooked through but they don't really dome. Remove the cakes from the oven and allow them to cool for about 5 minutes.

Sift the powdered sugar on the tops and decorate with the coffee beans. These cakes are best enjoyed day of but can be covered with plastic wrap and stored at room temperature about 3 days.

¼ cup coconut sugar

¼ cup heavy cream or milk of choice

1 tablespoon vegetable oil or melted butter

1 egg

¾ cup blanched almond flour

1 tablespoon instant espresso powder

¼ teaspoon baking soda

¼ teaspoon salt

1 tablespoon powdered sugar

4+ chocolate-covered coffee beans

MAKES 4 MINI CAKES
PREP: 5 MINUTES
BAKE: 20 MINUTES

Boston Cream Loaf Cake

When I was a kid, my mom would plop me in the front seat of a grocery cart and make a beeline to the bakery. Call it priorities, call it bribery, all I know is I got to happily sit and eat my donut while my mom shopped for groceries. Every single time, I would choose a Boston cream and deem it my "old favorite," even though there were no new favorites and it was, in fact, my only favorite. I'm revisiting my "old favorite" with this loaf cake. It hits all those layers of decadence I love, but made easier in a bread pan.

FOR THE CAKE

4 tablespoons unsalted butter, melted

3 tablespoons agave nectar, honey, or pure maple syrup

½ teaspoon pure vanilla extract

2 eggs

½ cup oat flour

1 teaspoon baking powder

½ teaspoon salt

FOR THE CREAM

4 egg yolks

¾ cup whole milk

¼ cup agave nectar, honey, or pure maple syrup

1 teaspoon pure vanilla extract

1 teaspoon arrowroot flour

1 tablespoon unsalted butter

FOR THE CHOCOLATE TOPPING

1 cup semisweet chocolate chips

2 tablespoons whole milk

2 tablespoons unsalted butter

MAKES 1 CAKE

PREP: 10 MINUTES +
50 MINUTES TOTAL CHILL TIME
BAKE: 20 MINUTES

Preheat the oven to 350°F. Line a 9-inch bread pan with parchment paper so that it lines the bottom and drapes over two sides of the pan.

To make the cake, in a large bowl, whisk together the butter, agave, vanilla, and eggs until combined. Add the oat flour, baking powder, and salt. Whisk again until smooth. Allow the batter to stand for about 2 minutes to thicken. Transfer the batter to the prepared pan. Use a rubber spatula to spread it out in an even layer.

Bake for 20 minutes, until the edges are golden brown and the center is set. Remove from the oven and allow it to cool completely in the pan.

To make the cream, while the cake cools, combine the egg yolks, milk, agave, vanilla, and arrowroot flour in a small saucepan over medium heat and whisk to combine. Cook, whisking constantly, for about 5 minutes, until the cream thickens. Remove from the heat and stir in the butter until melted.

Spread the cream on top of the cake (while still in the pan) and place plastic wrap on top, making sure it touches the cream so that a skin doesn't form. Chill in the fridge for 30 minutes to allow the cream layer to set.

To make the chocolate topping, in a small bowl, melt the chocolate chips, milk, and butter in the microwave, stirring every 30 seconds until smooth. (Alternatively, use a double boiler.) Whisk vigorously until it turns into a thick and glossy chocolate topping.

Remove the plastic wrap from the cake and gently spread the chocolate across the top in an even layer. Chill in the fridge for 20 minutes to allow the chocolate topping to set.

Slide a knife around the sides where the cake touches the pan, then pull the edges of the parchment paper to lift everything from the pan and place it on a serving plate. Cut into 8 slices.

Yogurt Streusel Coffee Cake

I'm stepping up classic coffee cake with whole-milk yogurt, which adds a moist and tender bounce. The yogurt also brings a creamy richness to the batter, resulting in an irresistible combination with the sweet crumble topping. I've seen coffee cakes with a very generous layer of the crumble to bring it to the next level. Feel free to double (or triple—is that crazy?) the topping to elevate your crumble.

FOR THE CAKE

2 eggs

4 tablespoons unsalted butter, melted

¼ cup plain whole-milk yogurt

¼ cup agave nectar, honey, or pure maple syrup

1 teaspoon pure vanilla extract

2 cups blanched almond flour

1 tablespoon instant espresso powder

2 teaspoons baking powder

½ teaspoon salt

FOR THE CRUMBLE

½ cup coconut sugar

2 tablespoons unsalted butter, melted

1 teaspoon ground cinnamon

MAKES 1 CAKE
PREP: 10 MINUTES
BAKE: 25 MINUTES

To make the cake, preheat the oven to 350°F. Line a 9-inch round or 8-inch square pan with parchment paper.

In a large bowl, whisk together the eggs, butter, yogurt, agave, and vanilla until combined. Add the almond flour, espresso powder, baking powder, and salt. Whisk again until incorporated. Transfer the batter to the prepared pan and spread it out in an even layer.

To make the crumble, combine the coconut sugar, butter, and cinnamon in a small bowl. Use your hands to scrunch the mixture to work the butter through the coconut sugar and create a lumpy crumble. Sprinkle the crumble on top of the batter.

Bake for 25 minutes, until the edges are golden brown and the center is set. Remove the cake from the oven and allow it to cool in the pan for at least 10 minutes before cutting into slices.

Pumpkin bread, pumpkin pie, and pumpkin spice lattes get a lot of hype. Although I'm more than happy to partake in these seasonal snacks, I feel like we're overlooking some other cozy options. For instance, sweet potato! This cake is moist, tender, and loaded with fragrant fall spices including cinnamon, ginger, and nutmeg. I call it snack cake because you'll probably break off a bite whenever you pass it during the day. If you want a not-too-sweet treat that complements your morning tea or afternoon coffee, this is it.

Preheat the oven to 350°F. Line a 9-inch square pan with parchment paper.

In a medium bowl, whisk together the sweet potato puree, ½ cup of coconut sugar, and the eggs until combined. Add the oat flour, baking powder, cinnamon, ginger, nutmeg, and salt. Whisk again until incorporated. Transfer the batter to the prepared pan. Use a rubber spatula to spread it out in an even layer.

In a small bowl, stir together the pecans and remaining ½ tablespoon of coconut sugar. Sprinkle it on top of the cake.

Bake for 20–22 minutes, until the center is set. Remove the cake from the oven and allow it to cool in the pan for about 5 minutes before cutting into 12 slices. Store leftover cake in an airtight container at room temperature for about 3 days or in the fridge for about 1 week.

Spiced Sweet Potato Snack Cake

½ cup sweet potato puree

½ cup + ½ tablespoon coconut sugar (divided)

2 eggs

1 cup oat flour

1 teaspoon baking powder

2 teaspoons ground cinnamon

1 teaspoon ground ginger

½ teaspoon ground nutmeg

½ teaspoon salt

½ cup chopped pecans

MAKES 1 CAKE
PREP: 10 MINUTES
BAKE: 20 MINUTES

Pies & Crisps

Pies aren't the first dessert to pop into my head. Honestly, they typically cross my mind just twice a year: Thanksgiving and summertime. It's unusual because pies are a big category of my favorite meal (dessert), and yet I tend to avoid making them. The truth is, I struggle with pies. I find them to be a bit intimidating, and they require a level of patience and perfection that removes some of the fun for me.

In this chapter, you won't find pies that require hours of prep or uniform pinching. Instead, you'll find fuss-free pies, rustic galettes, and casual crisps that are perfect for any occasion. These recipes are super approachable and give you tons of wiggle room to make mistakes.

You'll also find fruit! Compared with the other chapters, this one is bursting with fruity, juicy, jammy recipes. But, because I am the way that I am, I had to include all the nutty, chocolaty options as well.

Chocolate on Chocolate Brownie Pie

What's better than chocolate brownie pie? A double chocolate brownie pie! This fudgy brownie is baked in a chocolate cookielike crust, producing a deeply decadent dessert. Top with nuts, caramel sauce, or a dollop of whipped cream or ice cream to make this extra special.

FOR THE CRUST

4 tablespoons unsalted butter, melted

1 egg

1 cup blanched almond flour

¼ cup cocoa powder

¼ cup coconut sugar

¼ teaspoon salt

FOR THE BROWNIE

2 eggs

½ cup unsalted butter, melted

½ cup coconut sugar

2 tablespoons agave nectar, honey, or pure maple syrup

1 cup blanched almond flour

¼ cup cocoa powder

¼ teaspoon salt

⅓ cup chocolate chips of choice

Powdered sugar for sprinkling

MAKES 1 PIE
PREP: 20 MINUTES
BAKE: 25 MINUTES

To make the crust, preheat the oven to 350°F.

In a medium bowl, whisk together the butter and egg. Add the almond flour, cocoa powder, coconut sugar, and salt, then use a rubber spatula to fold and press everything together until a dough forms.

Transfer the dough to a 9-inch pie dish. Use damp hands to press the dough into the bottom and up the sides of the dish. The dough is super forgiving so don't feel like you're overworking it. Keep pressing and forming it into a crust. I think it's fun to leave the top a bit rustic and crumbly, but you can press down the top to make it a more uniform crust. Set aside.

To make the brownie, in a large bowl, whisk together the eggs, butter, coconut sugar, and agave until combined. Add the almond flour, cocoa powder, and salt. Whisk again until combined. Fold in the chocolate chips until they are incorporated. Transfer the brownie batter to the center of the crust and use a spatula to spread it out.

Bake for 25 minutes, until the center is set. Remove the pie from the oven and allow it to cool in the pan for about 15 minutes. Sift powdered sugar on top before cutting it into 8 slices.

Here she goes, busting out the Nutella again. I know, it's just so magical. These sweet little personal pies are hazelnut heaven. Allow the top to set for an hour or two and you'll get a silky-smooth mousse that plays beautifully off the texture of the nutty crust. For a thicker ganache you can really sink your teeth into, let the top set overnight.

To make the crust, preheat the oven to 400°F. Line a 12-cup muffin pan with small squares of parchment paper or liners.

Spread the hazelnuts on a baking sheet and roast for 12 minutes, until they begin to sweat and smell fragrant. Remove them from the oven and allow them to cool for 10 minutes. Set aside 12 hazelnuts (these will be the decorative topper) and transfer the rest to a food processor. Blitz the hazelnuts for about 10 seconds, until just slightly chopped up. Add the agave, butter, and salt and blitz them again for 20–30 seconds, until it turns into a chunky, mealy mixture in the processor.

Evenly divide the batter among the prepared cups. The crust mixture may look like it takes over the whole cup, but now we're going to pack it down. Use the back of a measuring cup to press the crust mixture into the bottom of the liners. Clean or wipe the measuring cup every few crusts to prevent the mixture from sticking. Once all the crusts are nice and packed down, set aside.

To make the ganache, place the chocolate hazelnut spread and butter in a large bowl. Use an electric mixer on medium speed to cream them together, about 2 minutes. Add the cream and mix on high speed for about 3 minutes, until the mixture appears fluffy. Transfer the ganache to a piping bag or a zip-top bag and cut off one corner (about ½ inch). Pipe the ganache in a circular motion to create a swirl on each nutty crust.

Top each pie with 1 of the 12 remaining hazelnuts and chill in the fridge for at least 1 hour. The hazelnut layer really sets in the fridge for a more fudgy texture.

Chocolate-Hazelnut Ganache Personal Pies

FOR THE CRUST

2 cups whole raw hazelnuts
+12 for decorating

2 tablespoons agave nectar, honey, or pure maple syrup

2 tablespoons unsalted butter, melted

½ teaspoon salt

FOR THE GANACHE

1 cup chocolate hazelnut spread, such as Nutella

4 tablespoons unsalted butter, softened

½ cup heavy cream

MAKES 12 PERSONAL PIES
PREP: 1 HOUR

Peanut Butter Chocolate Tart

I love when textures collide. This tart showcases a nutty peanut crust with a luxuriously creamy chocolate center. It's perfect for those who are fans of the classic combination of peanut butter and chocolate but want to indulge in a rich dessert. This tart is terrific for any occasion be it a fancy dinner party or an afternoon snack. I like a simple garnish of extra chopped peanuts, but be creative and try chopped chocolate peanut butter cups or dollops of whipped cream (or all the above).

FOR THE CRUST

2 cups unsalted roasted peanuts

2 tablespoons agave nectar

3 tablespoons refined coconut oil, melted (divided)

FOR THE CHOCOLATE FILLING

1¼ cups dark chocolate chips

¼ cup natural peanut butter

1 can (14 oz) unsweetened coconut cream

3 tablespoons agave nectar

1 teaspoon pure vanilla extract

¼ cup unsalted roasted peanuts, chopped

MAKES 1 TART

PREP: 15 MINUTES +
12+ HOURS CHILL TIME

To make the crust, place the peanuts in a food processor and process until they are chopped but still a little chunky. Add the agave and 2 tablespoons of coconut oil. Process until it balls up and is combined.

Grease a tart pan with the remaining 1 tablespoon of coconut oil. Dampen your hands and press the crust mixture into the bottom and up the sides of the prepared pan. Pop it in the fridge while you make the chocolate filling.

To make the chocolate filling, in a large bowl, stir together the chocolate chips and peanut butter.

In a small saucepan over medium heat, combine the coconut cream, agave, and vanilla. Stirring occasionally, bring the cream mixture to a boil. Remove it from the heat and pour it on top of the chocolate mixture. Allow everything to sit for about 2 minutes, then whisk until smooth.

Remove the pan from the fridge, then pour the chocolate mixture into the center of the crust and use a spatula to spread it out. Return it to the fridge for at least 3 hours. In my experience, leaving it overnight is the best!

When you're ready to eat, top the tart with the chopped peanuts and cut into 8 slices.

Banana Cream Pie Pudding Cups

After college, I worked in a law office for a couple of years. For one delicious day of employee appreciation, we brought in family favorite recipes to share. A banana cream pie was one I loved best. A creamy banana filling was layered with banana slices and graham cracker, plus whipped cream. It's one of those nostalgic desserts that instantly evokes running around barefoot at a summer barbecue. These pudding cups combine classic banana cream pie flavors with single-serve convenience, making them ideal for parties, potlucks, or weeknight sweet treats. Top with personal touches like chocolate shavings, caramel sauce, or chopped nuts.

2 very ripe bananas, mashed (about 1 cup mashed)

1⅓ cups whole milk

¼ cup arrowroot flour

¼ cup agave nectar

1 teaspoon pure vanilla extract

12 vanilla cookies, such as Nilla Wafers, or gluten-free pecan shortbread cookies

1 cup whipped cream or peanut butter whip from Peanut Butter Dream Trifle (page 81)

12 banana chips

MAKES 6 PUDDING CUPS
PREP: 5 MINUTES
COOK: 5 MINUTES

Place the mashed bananas, milk, arrowroot flour, agave, and and vanilla in a blender. Blend until the mixture reaches your desired consistency (I like it smooth).

Pour the banana mixture into a medium saucepan over medium heat. Cook, whisking constantly, for 5 minutes, until the mixture thickens. Remove the pudding from the heat and allow it to cool.

Break apart the cookies and portion into servings (I use about 2 cookies per serving). Layer the cookies, whipped cream, and banana pudding into 6 small serving dishes reserving a few cookie pieces and some whipped cream for garnish. I like using little glass cups so you can see the layers. Top each with whipped cream, a crumble of the cookie, and 2 banana chips.

This ice cream pie can take any form. Press the crust into a pie dish, square baking pan, bread pan, or muffin pan and then top with your favorite ice cream. The crust features the rich and nutty flavor of ground pistachios, mixed with sugar and butter. The center of the pie can also be customized with your favorite ice cream. I tend to err on the side of a smooth, plain option like vanilla so the chunky pistachios can really shine through.

Place the pistachios and almond flour in a food processor or blender. Process for about 10 seconds, until chopped up and mealy. Add the butter, agave, and coconut sugar. Process again until the pistachio mixture begins to clump together.

Take the ice cream out of the freezer and allow it to soften for a few minutes so you can spread it easily.

Meanwhile, transfer the pistachio mixture to a 9-inch pie dish and press it into the bottom and up the sides. You can take extra care to press down the edges to give it a cleaner look, but I like how the crumbly edge looks a bit rustic.

Scoop the ice cream into the center of the pie and use the back of a spoon to press it into an even layer across the bottom.

Cover the pie dish with aluminum foil and store and freeze for at least 3 hours. Cut into 8 slices.

Ice Cream Pie with Crunchy Pistachio Crust

2 cups salted roasted pistachios

½ cup blanched almond flour

4 tablespoons unsalted butter, melted

¼ cup agave nectar, honey, or pure maple syrup

2 tablespoons coconut sugar

1 pint pistachio ice cream or ice cream of choice (vanilla, chocolate, or my favorite, honeycomb)

MAKES 1 PIE

PREP: 10 MINUTES +
3+ HOURS CHILL TIME

My namesake! I called my blog The Toasted Pine Nut because at the time, in 2014, I was loving hard on pine nuts in one particular avocado-kale salad. How could these little bits of buttery nut impart so much flavor and pizzazz? While raw pine nuts are delicious, there is something magical that happens when you toast them. Pine nuts can be pricey, so I bought a giant bulk bag and am making them last. For an intensely indulgent dessert, try this pie—each bite is worth every penny.

To make the crust, preheat the oven to 350°F. Grease a 9-inch pie dish with butter or your favorite baking spray.

In a large bowl, whisk together the butter and egg until combined. Add the almond flour, arrowroot flour, and salt, then use a rubber spatula to fold and press everything together until a dough forms.

Transfer the dough to the prepared pie dish. Use your hands to press it into the bottom and up the sides of the dish. This will take some time to get right, and if needed, you can dampen your hands to help move the crust along. Don't get too stressed about keeping the dough intact. You can really press this into any shape you want. Use a fork to poke holes into the bottom of the dough.

Bake for 10 minutes, until the edges are just lightly golden. Remove the crust from the oven (but keep the oven on).

To make the filling, while the crust bakes, place the toasted pine nuts in a large bowl and set aside.

Continues on page 122

Sticky Caramel Pine Nut Pie

FOR THE CRUST

4 tablespoons unsalted butter, melted

1 egg

1 cup blanched almond flour

¼ cup arrowroot flour

½ teaspoon salt

FOR THE FILLING

2 cups pine nuts, toasted
(see note on page 122)

½ cup unsalted butter

⅔ cup coconut sugar

¼ cup agave nectar, honey,
or pure maple syrup

1 teaspoon pure vanilla extract

½ teaspoon salt

1 egg

1 tablespoon water

MAKES 1 PIE
PREP: 30 MINUTES
BAKE: 22 MINUTES

Continued from page 121

Place the butter in a medium saucepan over medium-low heat, stirring constantly, until the butter begins to foam and bubble, 5–8 minutes. Once light brown specks form at the bottom of the pan and the butter smells nutty, stop stirring and add the coconut sugar, agave, vanilla, and salt. Increase the heat to medium-high and bring to a rolling boil, whisking frequently for about 5 minutes, until the mixture thickens.

Pour the mixture into the bowl with the pine nuts. Use a rubber spatula to mix until the pine nuts are coated with the browned butter mixture. Transfer the pine nut mixture into the center of the crust. Use a spatula to spread it out in an even layer.

In a small bowl, whisk together the egg and water to make an egg wash. Use a kitchen brush to paint the crust edges with the egg wash.

Bake for 12–15 minutes, until the crust edges are golden brown. Remove the pie from the oven and allow it to cool completely before cutting it into 8 slices.

NOTE: *To toast the pine nuts, place them in a medium skillet over medium-low heat and toast them, stirring constantly, for about 10 minutes, until they begin to sweat, are golden brown, and smell heavenly. Do not look away—your pine nuts will burn. For this recipe, I recommend toasting the nuts before starting your crust.*

This galette isn't overly sweet and allows those juicy cherries to shine. Serve each slice with a dollop of vanilla ice cream or whipped cream, if you like.

Cherry Galette

Preheat the oven to 400°F.

To make the crust, in a large bowl, whisk together the the butter, vanilla, and egg until combined. Add the almond flour, arrowroot flour, and salt, then use a rubber spatula to fold and press everything together until a dough forms.

Place the dough between 2 large pieces of parchment paper. Use a rolling pin to roll out the dough to a ⅛-inch thickness. Slide a cutting board or baking sheet under the bottom parchment paper and freeze the dough while you make the filling.

To make the filling, place the cherries, agave, vanilla, and arrowroot flour in a large saucepan over medium-high heat and whisk to combine. Cook, stirring occasionally, for 15–20 minutes, until the cherry mixture has reduced and the liquid around the cherries becomes syrupy.

When the filling is ready, remove the dough from the freezer and transfer it to a baking sheet. Peel off the top layer of parchment paper and discard it. Add the cherry filling to the center of the dough. Use the bottom parchment paper to gently fold the edges of the crust into the center of the galette, leaving the middle open to expose the cherry filling. Make sure to fold the crust slowly so it doesn't crack at the folds. I typically make 4–5 folds so not to overwork the crust.

In a small bowl, whisk together the egg and water to paint the outer crust with the egg wash. Use a kitchen brush to paint the egg wash on the outer crust of the galette.

Bake for 15–20 minutes, until the crust is golden brown. Remove the galette from the oven and allow it to cool for 10 minutes. Sprinkle the galette with powdered sugar before cutting it into 6–8 slices. Serve with a scoop of vanilla ice cream.

FOR THE CRUST

4 tablespoons unsalted butter, melted

1 teaspoon vanilla bean paste

1 egg

1 cup blanched almond flour

¼ cup arrowroot flour

½ teaspoon salt

FOR THE FILLING

3 cups frozen pitted cherries

4 tablespoons agave nectar, honey, or pure maple syrup

1 teaspoon pure vanilla bean paste

½ teaspoon arrowroot flour

1 egg

1 tablespoon water

½ teaspoon powdered sugar

MAKES 1 GALETTE
PREP: 20 MINUTES
BAKE: 15 MINUTES

Sweet Oat Strawberry Galette

I love the rustic feel and personal touch of a galette. No two are folded the same, giving each its own personality. Once you try this galette crust, you'll want to experiment with different fillings. While sweets are always on my mind, the crust is perfect for savory fillings, too! Try adding some sliced tomatoes, spinach, and artichoke hearts, or caramelized onions and mushrooms, to the center of your galette for a delicious main dish.

4 tablespoons unsalted butter

2 tablespoons coconut sugar

1 egg

1 cup blanched almond flour

¼ cup arrowroot flour

3 tablespoons gluten-free rolled oats, divided

½ teaspoon salt

2 tablespoons strawberry jam

About 20 strawberries, halved

1 egg + 1 tablespoon water, beaten together in a small bowl

1 tablespoon turbinado sugar

2 tablespoons agave nectar, honey, or pure maple syrup

Vanilla ice cream or whipped cream for serving (optional)

MAKES 1 GALETTE

PREP: 30 MINUTES
BAKE: 15 MINUTES

Preheat the oven to 400°F.

Place the butter in a medium bowl and soften it in the microwave for about 30 seconds. Add the coconut sugar, egg, almond flour, arrowroot flour, 2 tablespoons of oats, and the salt, then use a rubber spatula to fold and press everything together until a dough forms.

Place the dough bewteen 2 large pieces of parchment paper and roll it out in a round shape about ⅛ inch thick. Slide a cutting board or baking sheet underneath the bottom piece of parchment paper and place in the freezer for about 20 minutes.

Remove the dough from the freezer and transfer it to a baking sheet. Peel off the top layer of parchment and discard it.

Spread the strawberry jam on the center of the dough. Arrange the strawberries on top of the jam in the center of the dough, leaving a 2-inch border. Use the bottom parchment paper to gently fold the edges of the crust into the center of the galette, leaving the middle open to expose the strawberries. Make sure to fold the crust slowly so it doesn't crack at the folds. I typically make 4–5 folds to create a square or circle shape so not to overwork the crust.

Use a kitchen brush to paint the outer crust with the egg wash. Sprinkle with the turbinado sugar and the remaining 1 tablespoon of oats.

Bake for 15 minutes, until the crust is golden brown. The edges of the galette may crack a bit, but that's okay. It will hold together and firm up as it cools. Remove the galette from the oven. Drizzle the filling with the agave and allow it to cool for 20 minutes. Cut the galette into 4–6 slices and serve with vanilla ice cream (if using).

I remember my mom once ordering a little handheld apple pie at a drive-through, and I couldn't get over it. Adorable! Convenient! Delicious! I love the single-serve, dessert to go, with folks all getting their own personal treat. Substitute your favorite cherry, berry, nutty, or chocolate pie filling to make hand pies to suit any occasion.

To make the crust, preheat the oven to 350°F. Line 2 baking sheets with parchment paper.

In a large bowl, whisk together the egg, butter, agave, and vanilla until combined. Add the almond flour, arrowroot flour, and salt, then use a rubber spatula to fold and press together until a dough forms.

Place the dough between 2 large pieces of parchment paper. Use a rolling pin to roll out the dough to a ¼-inch thickness. Slide a cutting board or baking sheet under the bottom parchment paper and freeze the dough while you make the filling.

To make the filling, in a large saucepan over medium-high heat, combine the butter, agave, coconut sugar, vanilla, cinnamon, salt, arrowroot flour, and apples. Bring to a rolling boil and cook, stirring frequently, for 15–20 minutes, until the apples are tender and the caramel syrup around the fruit reduces. Set aside.

Remove the dough from the freezer and peel off the top layer of parchment paper and discard it.

Continues on page 128

Apple-Cinnamon Hand Pies

FOR THE CRUST

1 egg

⅓ cup unsalted butter, melted

¼ cup agave nectar

1 teaspoon pure vanilla extract

2 cups blanched almond flour

½ cup arrowroot flour

½ teaspoon salt

FOR THE FILLING

½ cup unsalted butter

½ cup agave nectar

2 tablespoons coconut sugar

1 teaspoon pure vanilla extract

1 teaspoon ground cinnamon

½ teaspoon salt

¼ teaspoon arrowroot flour

3 Honeycrisp apples, peeled, cored, and small cubed

1 egg

1 tablespoon water

Turbinado sugar for sprinkling

MAKES 8 HAND PIES
PREP: 20 MINUTES
BAKE: 13 MINUTES PER BATCH

Continued from page 127

To make the hand pies, work in batches. Use a 4- to 5-inch bowl to cut out 4 circles of dough. Use a sturdy rubber spatula to lift the circles and transfer them to one of the prepared baking sheets. Spoon about 1 tablespoon of the filling in the center of each dough circle, making sure to leave room around the edges. Fold one side of the dough over on top of the other side. Use a fork to press and seal the edges.

In a small bowl, whisk together the egg and water to paint the top of each pie. Use a kitchen brush to paint the top of each pie with the egg wash, then sprinkle with turbinado sugar.

Bake for about 13 minutes, until the tops are golden brown. Remove the pies from the oven and allow them to cool for about 10 minutes before transferring them to a wire rack.

While the first batch of hand pies is baking, gather the dough scraps and reroll out between 2 pieces of parchment paper to a ¼-inch thickness. Set on a flat surface and return it to the freezer for 10 minutes before starting on your second batch. Then, repeat the assembly and baking process.

I love making nutty fruit crisps because they play off an iconic childhood sandwich combo—peanut butter and jelly. Here I'm adding pecans and almond flour to the traditional oats to create a super-crumbly crisp that pairs well with the juicy berries. My favorite way to eat this is with a heaping scoop of vanilla ice cream, letting it melt into the berry crisp. Each spoonful oozes with creamy, nutty, juicy bursts that will have you coming back for more.

To make the crumble, preheat the oven to 350°F.

Place the pecans, almond flour, coconut sugar, and salt in a food processor. Process for a few seconds to combine and chop the pecans a bit. Add the peanut butter, butter, and vanilla and process again until the crumble starts to ball up. If needed, scrape down the sides and process for another 5 seconds. Add the oats and pulse a few times to incorporate and slightly chop the oats. Set the crumble aside.

To make the berry filling, in a medium saucepan over high heat, combine the berries, coconut sugar, vanilla, and cinnamon. Cook, stirring, for about 10 minutes, until the berries reduce and the filling becomes syrupy.

Press a handful of the crumble into the bottom of each of 4 ramekins in a compact, even layer, saving some crumble for topping. Divide the berry filling among the ramekins. Top each with the reserved crumble. Place the ramekins on a baking sheet.

Bake for 15 minutes, until the crisps are fragrantly nutty and slightly golden on top. Top with vanilla ice cream.

Super-Crumbly Mixed Berry Crisps

FOR THE CRUMBLE

1 cup raw pecans

1 cup blanched almond flour

2 tablespoons coconut sugar

¼ teaspoon salt

¼ cup natural peanut butter or nut butter of choice

4 tablespoons unsalted butter, melted

1 teaspoon pure vanilla extract

½ cup gluten-free rolled oats

FOR THE BERRY FILLING

3 cups frozen mixed berries

¼ cup coconut sugar

1 teaspoon pure vanilla extract

½ teaspoon ground cinnamon

Vanilla ice cream for serving

MAKES 4 CRISPS
PREP: 15 MINUTES
BAKE: 15 MINUTES

No Bake

While no-bake desserts are great any time of year—the ease! the simplicity!—I have a particular love for them in the summer months. When my kids were babies, we lived in an old Philly townhome with minimal air-conditioning. I have a distinct memory of being so sweaty and sticky during those hot summers that turning on the oven was not an option. Still wanting that sweet fix, I began to adore no-bake treats because they usually call for only a few ingredients and can be made in about ten minutes. Plus, they tend to be very kid friendly, allowing for helping hands of all sizes.

No-bake desserts are often very forgiving too. If you're a bit overwhelmed by baking, want an easy and totally doable recipe, or just need something quick and sweet to throw together, you've found a great chapter. It's filled with recipes that can take you from a holiday dinner to a casual bake sale.

Pistachio Freezer Fudge

At one point, I gifted my parents a special pistachio bowl set. A smaller bowl sits inside a larger bowl, one for full pistachios and one for shells. They laughed at first, thinking it was a gag gift. A week later, they told me how useful it was. My point is, we're pistachio people. Pistachio people to the point that we need a special setup for our nuts. Typically, I'm perfectly happy to eat pistachios in their original form, but I thought it would be tasty to make them into something a bit more decadent. This freezer fudge is only "fudge" in the sense it has that same sink-your-teeth-into texture. The ingredients are streamlined, and the flavor is delightfully satisfying.

1 cup roasted, salted shelled pistachios

1 cup (8 oz) white chocolate chips or white chocolate bars

1 teaspoon refined coconut oil

Flaky salt for sprinkling

MAKES 12 SQUARES

PREP: 5 MINUTES +
30+ MINUTES CHILL TIME

Line a 9-inch bread pan with parchment paper so that it lines the bottom and drapes over two sides of the pan. I find it easiest to clip the sides of the pan with chip clips or clothespins to make sure the parchment paper doesn't fall.

Place the pistachios in a food processor. Pulse for about 30 seconds, until chopped up but still chunky. Don't overprocess! You don't want it to turn into meal.

In a small bowl, melt the chocolate in the microwave, stirring every 30 seconds, until smooth. (Alternatively, use a double boiler.) Add the coconut oil and pistachios and stir until combined.

Transfer the chocolate pistachio mixture to the prepared pan and use a rubber spatula to spread it out in an even layer. Chill in the fridge for 30 minutes to 1 hour, until the chocolate hardens.

Remove the pan from the fridge. Pull the edges of the parchment paper to lift everything from the pan and place it on a cutting board. Allow it to sit on the cutting board for about 5 minutes before using a sharp knife to cut 12 squares. Sprinkle with flaky salt. Store in an airtight container in the fridge for up to 2 weeks.

Discovering puffed quinoa sent me down a path of no-bake recipes that have quickly become some of my go-to recipes. These peanut butter bars are a cross between your favorite peanut butter cups and crispy treats. They come together quickly and are easy to adapt into any shape. Cut them into long granola bar–style rectangles instead of squares, roll the peanut butter mixture into balls, or press it into a muffin pan.

Line a 9-inch bread pan with parchment paper.

In a large bowl, whisk together the peanut butter and agave until smooth. Fold in the puffed quinoa until incorporated. Transfer the mixture to the prepared pan. Press it down until it's an even layer on the bottom.

In a small bowl, melt the chocolate chips in the microwave, stirring every 30 seconds until smooth. (Alternatively, use a double boiler.) Add the coconut oil and stir until completely smooth. Pour the chocolate on top of the crispy peanut butter layer and spread in an even layer. Chill in the freezer for 2 hours, until hardened.

Remove the pan from the freezer and use a sharp knife to cut into 8 squares. Sprinkle with flaky salt and store in an airtight container in the fridge for up to 1 week.

Crispy Peanut Butter Bars

1½ cups natural peanut butter

¼ cup agave nectar, honey, or pure maple syrup

1½ cups puffed quinoa

½ cup chocolate chips of choice

1 tablespoon refined coconut oil

Flaky salt for sprinkling

MAKES 8 SQUARES

PREP: 10 MINUTES +
2 HOURS CHILL TIME

Layered Chocolate Mint Bars

For a big part of my life, I ate York peppermint patties in a very meticulous, routine way: I'd nibble around the circumference and then plunge the entire remaining circle into my mouth and savor that minty cream middle. The combination of cool mint and rich chocolate is reminiscent of those peppermint patties and Andes Candies. Aside from their creamy mint layer, I love how simple these bars are to make. They are no bake, take almost no time to assemble, and can be stored in your fridge or freezer for whenever you want a treat to brighten your day.

1 cup semisweet chocolate chips

1 tablespoon refined coconut oil

½ cup coconut butter

¼ cup agave nectar, honey, or pure maple syrup

2 teaspoons mint extract

1 drop green food coloring (optional)

MAKES 16 BARS

PREP: 15 MINUTES +
15 MINUTES CHILL TIME

Line a 9-inch bread pan with parchment paper so that it lines the bottom and drapes over two sides of the pan.

In a small bowl, melt the chocolate chips and coconut oil in the microwave, stirring every 30 seconds until smooth. (Alternatively, use a double boiler.) Pour half of the chocolate mixture into the prepared pan and spread in an even layer. Chill in the fridge or freezer for 5 minutes, until the chocolate hardens.

In a medium bowl, whisk together the coconut butter, agave, mint extract, and food coloring (if using). The mixture should thicken up and some white coconut liquid may separate (that's okay!). Pour out and discard any liquid that doesn't incorporate. Transfer the mint mixture to the pan and spread it out in an even layer on top of the hardened chocolate layer.

Pour the remaining chocolate mixture on top of the mint layer and spread in an even layer. Chill in the fridge or freezer for 10 minutes, until the chocolate hardens.

Remove the pan from the fridge or freezer. Pull the edges of the parchment paper to lift everything from the pan and place it on a cutting board. Use a large knife to cut into 16 bars. Enjoy or store in an airtight container at room temperature or in the fridge for up to 2 weeks.

No-Bake Chocolate Peanut Butter Bars

FOR THE PEANUT BUTTER LAYER

1 cup natural peanut butter

½ cup refined coconut oil, melted

¼ cup agave nectar

½ teaspoon salt

FOR THE CHOCOLATE LAYER

½ cup chocolate chips of choice

2 tablespoons natural peanut butter

1 tablespoon refined coconut oil

Flaky salt for sprinkling (optional)

MAKES 8 BARS

PREP: 30 MINUTES +
1 HOUR CHILL TIME

No-bake recipes are perfect for stashing away in the back of the fridge or freezer because they keep for weeks and you can enjoy one whenever your sweet tooth strikes. I love the peanut butter and chocolate combo (always and forever), but feel free to sub in almond butter, tahini, or even sunflower seed butter to switch up the flavor!

To make the peanut butter layer, line a 9-inch bread pan with parchment paper so that it lines the bottom and drapes over two sides of the pan.

In a large bowl, whisk together the peanut butter, coconut oil, agave, and salt until smooth. Transfer the peanut butter mixture to the prepared pan and use a rubber spatula to spread it out in an even layer. Chill in the freezer for 10 minutes while you prep the chocolate layer.

To make the chocolate layer, in a medium bowl, melt the chocolate chips in the microwave, stirring every 30 seconds until smooth. (Alternatively, use a double boiler.) Add the peanut butter and coconut oil and whisk until combined.

Remove the pan from the freezer and pour the chocolate mixture on top of the peanut butter layer, then sprinkle with flaky salt (if using). Chill the bars in the freezer for about 1 hour, until the chocolate hardens.

Remove the pan from the freezer. Pull the edges of the parchment paper to lift everything from the pan and place it on a cutting board. Use a large knife to cut into 8 bars. Store in an airtight container in the fridge for up to 2 weeks.

Holy texture! I love when contrasting textures get together for one big party. The creamy peanut butter base of these bars is loaded with chopped almonds, chocolate chips, shredded coconut, and flaxseed, making for a super-chunky, crunchy contrast. And those add-ins are packed with nutrients like protein and fiber. Store these bars in the fridge and grab one anytime. Be forewarned—they soften at room temperature, so they're not ideal for on the go.

Line a 9-inch bread pan with parchment paper so that it lines the bottom and drapes over two sides of the pan.

In a large bowl, whisk together the peanut butter, coconut oil, agave, vanilla, and salt until smooth and combined. Use a rubber spatula to fold in the almonds, chocolate chips, coconut, and flaxseed.

Transfer the batter to the prepared pan and use the rubber spatula to smooth it out in an even layer. Sprinkle the top with additional almonds and chocolate chips. Chill in the freezer for about 2 hours, until the bars harden and are firm to the touch.

Remove the pan from the freezer. Pull the edges of the parchment paper to lift everything from the pan and and place it on a cutting board. Use a large knife to cut into 8 bars. Store in an airtight container in the fridge for up to 2 weeks.

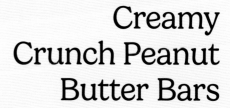

Creamy Crunch Peanut Butter Bars

1 cup natural peanut butter

3 tablespoons refined coconut oil, melted

3 tablespoons agave nectar

½ teaspoon pure vanilla extract

Pinch sea salt

½ cup almonds, chopped + more for topping

½ cup dark chocolate chips + more for topping

¼ cup unsweetened shredded coconut

¼ cup flaxseed

MAKES 8 BARS

PREP: 10 MINUTES + 2 HOURS CHILL TIME

Cookie Butter

Have you had those Biscoff cookies on an airplane? Or bought (and eaten an entire jar of) Trader Joe's cookie butter? This recipe was born into the same family as those delicious delicacies. There's something about it that leaves your mouth watering for another taste. I'm a big fan of eating this bite for bite with a spoon, but if you're looking for variety, add a scoop to your ice cream, spread it across a slice of cinnamon toast or pancakes, or use it in the Cookie Butter Cake with Sweet Whipped Butter (page 88).

Place the graham crackers in a food processor and process until chopped up into a sandy texture. Add the butter, agave, vanilla, cinnamon, and salt. Process again until incorporated, stopping to scrape down the sides of the food processor with a rubber spatula as needed. Process until the cookie butter is just combined and reaches your desired texture (in my opinion, less is more!). Over-processing it will make the mixture ball up and become doughy.

Store in an airtight container at room temperature for 3 days or in the fridge for about 1 week. Dip, dunk, or spoon onto whatever you like!

9 gluten-free graham crackers (1 pack)

4 tablespoons unsalted butter, melted

¼ cup agave nectar, honey, or pure maple syrup

1 teaspoon pure vanilla extract

½ teaspoon ground cinnamon

½ teaspoon salt

MAKES 1½ CUPS

PREP: 5 MINUTES

Mocha Ganache Topped with Fluffy Meringue

This make-ahead dessert is the love child of two of my favorite things: s'mores and coffee. The chocolate ganache is infused with espresso and topped with a fluffy Italian meringue. It's fun to serve this in small glasses, but teacups, ramekins, or little bowls make for a festive treat! Garnish with some graham crackers for an elevated campfire flair.

FOR THE GANACHE

1¼ cups semisweet chocolate chips

4 tablespoons unsalted butter

2 cups unsweetened coconut cream

3 tablespoons agave nectar

2 tablespoons instant espresso powder

1 teaspoon pure vanilla extract

FOR THE MERINGUE

2 egg whites

¼ cup agave nectar

2 gluten-free graham crackers

Cocoa powder for garnish (optional)

SERVES 6

PREP: 35 MINUTES +
24 HOURS CHILL TIME

To make the ganache, place the chocolate chips and butter in a large bowl.

In a small saucepan over medium-high heat, whisk together the coconut cream, agave, espresso powder, and vanilla. Bring to a simmer, stirring frequently for everything to be evenly combined. Remove the mixture from the heat and pour it into the bowl with the chocolate chip mixture. Allow the contents to sit in the bowl for a few minutes, then whisk the ganache until silky smooth.

Divide the ganache among 6 small ramekins or glass cups. Chill in the fridge overnight or for 24 hours.

To make the meringue, once the ganache is chilled, place the egg whites in a medium bowl. Use an electric mixer on high speed to whip the egg whites for about 3 minutes, until soft peaks form. You'll know you have soft peaks when you lift your mixer and the egg white forms a small little mountain with a "peak" that then melts back down into itself fairly quickly.

Place the agave nectar in a small saucepan over medium-high heat until it begins to simmer. Continue to whip the egg whites with your mixer and slowly pour in the hot agave. Be careful not to splatter. Continue to whip for about 5 minutes, until firm peaks form. You'll know you have firm peaks when you lift your mixer and the egg white peaks are stiff, upright, and don't fall back into themselves.

Transfer the meringue to a piping bag or a zip-top bag and cut off one corner (about ½ inch). Swirl the fluff around the top of the ganache in a circular motion. Break the graham crackers into smaller rectangular pieces. Add a graham cracker pieces to the side of each serving. Crush the remaining graham cracker and sprinkle it on top of each. Sift cocoa powder (if using) on top.

Another recipe I found in my grandmom's recipe binder was for rocky road clusters. I've always adored no-bake desserts and was thrilled to discover my love may be genetic. I've switched up her original recipe by pulsing the pecans and marshmallows in a food processor before forming chocolaty mounds and finishing them off with flaky salt. I think she'd approve!

In a large bowl, melt the chocolate chips in the microwave, stirring every 30 seconds until smooth. (Alternatively, use a double boiler.)

Place the pecans and marshmallows in a food processor. Pulse until just chopped and combined. Add the pecan mixture to the chocolate and fold together until everything is coated with chocolate.

Line a baking sheet or cutting board with parchment paper. Use a cookie scoop or 2 tablespoons to drop small dollops of the mixture onto the prepared baking sheet. You should have about 16 clusters.

Sprinkle with flaky salt and chill in the fridge for 15 minutes, until the chocolate hardens, before serving.

Rocky Road Clusters

1 cup chocolate chips of choice

1 cup chopped pecans

1 cup mini marshmallows

Flaky salt for sprinkling

MAKES 16 CLUSTERS

PREP: 10 MINUTES +
15 MINUTES CHILL TIME

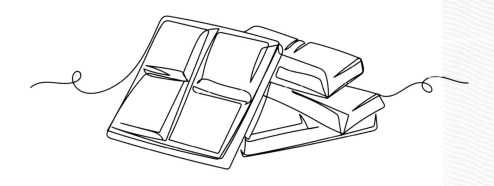

Salted Caramel Chews

The only thing I don't love about store-bought caramel squares is the little plastic wrapper that makes you work too hard. In the event that you, too, are done with those torture folds, make your own candies to have on hand for whenever you want to indulge or need caramels to use in a recipe. They are soft, chewy, and perfectly bite-size. Wrap them individually in easy parchment-paper twists and store them in the back of your fridge.

½ cup unsweetened coconut cream

½ cup agave nectar, honey, or pure maple syrup

2 tablespoons coconut sugar

½ teaspoon pure vanilla extract

½ teaspoon salt

¼ teaspoon arrowroot flour

Flaky salt for sprinkling

MAKES 15–18 CANDIES
PREP: 5 MINUTES +
3 HOURS CHILL TIME
COOK: 10 MINUTES

In a medium saucepan over high heat, combine the coconut cream, agave, coconut sugar, vanilla, and salt. Place a sifter over the pan and sift the arrowroot flour into the mixture, whisking to make sure it doesn't clump. Bring to a boil and cook, whisking frequently, for about 10 minutes, until the mixture thickens and lightens in color.

Transfer to a medium bowl or dish and allow it to come to room temperature. Cover the bowl with a lid, aluminum foil, or plastic wrap and chill the caramel in the fridge for 3 hours, until hardened but still malleable.

Prep small rectangles of parchment paper to wrap up your chews. Use a teaspoon to scoop some of the caramel into your hands and roll it into a log. Place the candy on a parchment rectangle, sprinkle with flaky salt, and roll the candy in the parchment, twisting off the ends. Continue this process until all the caramel is made into individual candies. You may need to wash your hands throughout this process as it can become a bit greasy.

Store the caramel chews in a bag or container in the fridge for up to 2 weeks.

Almond Joys

I had a standard approach to eating Almond Joys as a kid. First, I'd nibble off all the chocolate. Then I'd pluck away the almond and eat that, too. Finally, I'd bite into the coconut and savor every second we got to spend together. Over the years, I've tried to perfect my own version, and the key is using coconut butter. It helps bind that shredded coconut with a soft, creamy base.

1 cup unsweetened shredded coconut

½ cup coconut butter, melted

¼ cup agave nectar, honey, or pure maple syrup

¼ teaspoon salt

14 whole raw almonds

1 cup semisweet chocolate chips

1 tablespoon refined coconut oil

MAKES 14 CANDIES

PREP: 20 MINUTES + 20 MINUTES CHILL TIME

Line a baking sheet or cutting board with parchment paper.

In a large bowl, stir together the coconut, coconut butter, agave, and salt until combined. Use your hands to take ½–1 tablespoon of the coconut mixture and form oval mounds, placing them on the prepared baking sheet. Press 1 almond on top of each mound. Chill in the fridge for about 10 minutes, until set.

While the mounds are chilling, in a small bowl, melt the chocolate chips in the microwave, stirring every 30 seconds until smooth. (Alternatively, use a double boiler.) Add the coconut oil and stir until the chocolate is gorgeously drizzly.

Move the coconut mounds to one side of the baking sheet. On the other side, place a rack on top of the parchment paper. Place the mounds on the rack and use a spoon to coat them with melted chocolate. Alternatively, place the mounds directly into the chocolate bowl and use a fork to coat them with chocolate, allowing any excess chocolate to drip away. Then place them on the rack.

Chill the candies in the freezer for about 10 minutes, until the chocolate is hardened. Store in an airtight container at room temperature until you're ready to eat. If it's summer or hot where you live, you may want to store them in the fridge so they don't melt before you can eat them. The candies will keep for about 2 weeks.

When I lived in California, there was a local treat that I used to grab whenever I saw it in stores: Celebré peanut butter balls. These delightful candies had a cookie crunch that elevated them above a standard chocolate peanut butter cup. I borrowed that cookie crunch for these truffles by mixing graham cracker bits into the peanut butter. Then they are rolled into balls and bathed in a luscious chocolate coating. The result is a flavor and texture profile that's bound to be a hit everywhere.

In a large bowl, whisk together the peanut butter, agave, and vanilla until combined. Add the almond flour, salt, and crushed graham crackers. Fold until combined. Chill in the fridge for 15 minutes.

Line a baking sheet or cutting board with parchment paper. Using your hands, grab 1–2 tablespoons of the peanut butter mixture and form a ball or oval shape. Place on the prepared baking sheet. Chill in the fridge for about 15 minutes, until the truffles are firm to the touch and easily handled.

While the truffles are chilling, in a small bowl, melt the chocolate chips and coconut oil in the microwave, stirring every 30 seconds until smooth. (Alternatively, use a double boiler.)

Place each truffle on a fork and hold it over the chocolate bowl. Use a spoon to drizzle chocolate on top and use the back of the spoon to spread it smoothly. Return the chocolate-coated truffle to the baking sheet.

Sprinkle with flaky salt, then chill in the fridge for about 20 minutes, until the chocolate hardens. Enjoy immediately or store in an airtight container in the fridge for about 2 weeks.

Peanut Butter and Graham Cracker Truffles

½ cup natural peanut butter

⅓ cup agave nectar, honey, or pure maple syrup

1 teaspoon pure vanilla extract

½ cup blanched almond flour

¼ teaspoon salt

1 cup crushed gluten-free graham crackers (about 6 crackers)

1 cup semisweet chocolate chips

1 tablespoon refined coconut oil

Flaky salt for sprinkling

MAKES 12 TRUFFLES

PREP: 20 MINUTES +
50 MINUTES TOTAL CHILL TIME

Here I go with the tahini again. I'm telling you, once you bring tahini into your desserts, you'll think about it every time you start a recipe. Is tahini appropriate here? Can I squeeze it in somehow? This sesame seed paste adds an unexpected savory ribbon throughout.

Line a baking sheet or cutting board with parchment paper.

In a medium bowl, whisk together the tahini, agave, and vanilla until combined. Add the almond flour and pink salt, then use a rubber spatula to fold and press everything together until a dough forms. Add ⅓ cup of chocolate chips and fold until incorporated.

Use a cookie scoop to scoop 12 balls of the dough and roll them between your hands to smooth them out. Place on the prepared baking sheet.

In a small bowl, melt the remaining ⅔ cup of chocolate chips and the coconut oil in the microwave, stirring every 30 seconds until smooth. (Alternatively, use a double boiler.)

One at a time, drop each ball into the bowl to coat it with the chocolate. Return the chocolate-coated ball to the baking sheet. Sprinkle with flaky salt.

Chill in the fridge for at least 30 minutes, until the chocolate hardens. Store in an airtight container in the fridge for up to 2 weeks.

Tahini–Chocolate Chip Cookie Dough Truffles

½ cup tahini

¼ cup agave nectar, honey, or pure maple syrup

1 teaspoon pure vanilla extract

½ cup blanched almond flour

½ teaspoon pink salt

1 cup mini dark chocolate chips (divided)

1 tablespoon refined coconut oil

Flaky salt for sprinkle

MAKES 12 TRUFFLES

PREP: 10 MINUTES + 30+ MINUTES CHILL TIME

Chocolate Sprinkle Truffles

6 tablespoons unsweetened coconut cream

2 tablespoons agave nectar

1 teaspoon pure vanilla extract

1 cup semisweet chocolate chips

⅓ cup rainbow sprinkles

MAKES 12 TRUFFLES

PREP: 30 MINUTES +
1 HOUR CHILL TIME

These truffles combine a smooth, fudgy ganache center with a bright and colorful coating of rainbow sprinkles. The contrast in texture makes you cherish every bite. They're a convenient dessert option because you can prep and store them in the fridge until you're ready to serve. Want to switch it up? Roll the chocolate balls in chopped nuts (hazelnuts would be amazing!), powdered sugar, or chopped candies.

In a medium bowl, heat the coconut cream, agave, and vanilla in the microwave for 1 minute. (Alternatively, heat them together in a small saucepan over medium-high heat.) Add the chocolate chips and wait 1 minute for them to melt, then whisk everything together until smooth. Chill in the fridge for 1 hour, until the chocolate hardens into a dense fudge.

Place the rainbow sprinkles in a shallow bowl. Use a cookie scoop to scoop a ball of the hardened chocolate. Drop it into the bowl of sprinkles. Coat the ball with sprinkles, then roll it between your hands to smooth it out and to press the sprinkles into the surface of the truffle. Set it on a small serving plate and continue until all the chocolate is used up.

Store in an airtight container in the fridge for up to 2 weeks.

Monster Cookie Energy Balls

½ cup natural peanut butter

¼ cup agave nectar, honey, or pure maple syrup

⅔ cup blanched almond flour

⅔ cup gluten-free rolled oats

¼ cup candy-coated chocolate chips or mini M&M's

MAKES 12–14 BALLS

PREP: 10 MINUTES + 1+ HOUR CHILL TIME

I always wondered about the difference between monster cookies and kitchen sink cookies. I think it's that the former have a peanut butter base whereas the latter are buttery in texture. This is the perfect quick recipe to whip together and makes a great pick-me-up.

Line a plate with parchment paper.

In a medium bowl, whisk together the peanut butter and agave until combined. Add the almond flour, oats, and most of the chocolate chips, saving a few to press into the balls after rolling. Use a rubber spatula to fold everything together until incorporated.

Use a cookie scoop to scoop out 12–14 mounds of the dough. Roll each mound in your hands to form a smooth ball, then press some reserved chocolate chips into the outside.

Place the balls on the prepared plate and chill in the fridge for at least 1 hour, until set. Store in an airtight container in the fridge for up to 2 weeks.

The moment I found out you could melt chocolate, add in whatever you want, and call it bark was transformative. The possibilities! The irregular pieces! I have folded many combinations of goodies into my melty chocolate to make bark and worked tirelessly to perfect my ratios. Retesting chocolate bark recipes isn't the worst. This bark, with hazelnuts and crunchy quinoa, reminds me of the outside chocolate shell of a Ferrero Rocher candy. Be sure to buy the puffed quinoa that is crispy, not soft and puffy.

Line a baking sheet with parchment paper.

In a small bowl, melt the chocolate chips and coconut oil in the microwave, stirring every 30 seconds until smooth. (Alternatively, use a double boiler.) Use a rubber spatula to fold in the puffed quinoa and hazelnuts until combined. Transfer the chocolate mixture to the prepared baking sheet and spread it out in an even layer.

Sprinkle with the remaining 1 tablespoon of puffed quinoa (this is purely for aesthetics and not necessary to the recipe) and some flaky salt.

Chill the bark in the fridge for 1–2 hours, until hardened. Pull the edges of the parchment paper to lift the bark from the baking sheet and place it on a cutting board. Cut or break the bark into pieces. Enjoy immediately or store in an airtight container at room temperature for about 2 weeks.

Crispy Quinoa Hazelnut Chocolate Bark

12 oz chocolate chips of choice

2 tablespoons refined coconut oil

1 cup + 1 tablespoon puffed quinoa (divided)

½ cup chopped roasted salted hazelnuts

Flaky salt for sprinkling

MAKES 18 PIECES

PREP: 5 MINUTES +
1+ HOUR CHILL TIME

There's this trick with cheesecake that helps ensure it's smooth, creamy, and doesn't crack on top. It's called a water bath (or bain-marie). You put a pan of water underneath the cheesecake as it bakes. It feels a bit daunting, but chefs swear it's the way to achieve a perfect cheesecake. The great news is, you don't need anything of the sort for my cheesecake! This is the easiest no-bake one you'll ever come across. The cake itself only has three ingredients and is a great make-ahead dessert for any occasion.

To make the crust, in a large bowl, whisk together the peanut butter, agave, and vanilla until combined. Add the almond flour, salt, and most of the chocolate chips, saving about 1 tablespoon to sprinkle on the top of the cake. Use a rubber spatula to fold and press everything together until a dough forms. Chill the dough in the fridge while you prep the cheesecake.

To make the filling, in a medium bowl, whisk the cream cheese until smooth. Add the cream and agave and whisk for about 1 minute, until they are incorporated and whipped a bit.

Line an 8-inch springform pan with parchment paper. Transfer the chilled dough to the prepared pan and use your hands to press it into the bottom and up the sides. If the dough is a bit sticky, dampen your hands to help you spread it out in an even layer.

Add the filling to the center of the crust and use a rubber spatula to spread it out in an even layer. Sprinkle with the remaining 1 tablespoon of chocolate chips. Chill the cake in the freezer for at least 2 hours, until the center is firm to the touch.

Release the springform pan to remove the cake. Allow it to sit at room temperature for about 10 minutes before cutting it into 8 slices.

The Easiest Cheesecake with a Cookie Dough Crust

FOR THE CRUST

½ cup natural peanut butter

⅓ cup agave nectar, honey, or pure maple syrup

1 teaspoon pure vanilla extract

1 cup blanched almond flour

¼ teaspoon salt

½ cup mini chocolate chips

FOR THE FILLING

8 oz cream cheese, room temperature

⅓ cup heavy cream

¼ cup agave nectar, honey, or pure maple syrup

MAKES 1 CHEESECAKE

PREP: 10 MINUTES + 2+ HOURS CHILL TIME

Chocolate Peanut Butter Crunch Pie

2 cups semisweet chocolate chips

½ cup heavy cream

1 cup natural peanut butter

¼ cup agave nectar

1 teaspoon pure vanilla extract

¼ teaspoon salt

½ cup puffed quinoa

Flaky salt for sprinkling

MAKES 1 PIE

PREP: 15 MINUTES +
40 MINUTES TOTAL CHILL TIME

My goal for this crunch pie was to create a giant peanut butter cup. But after a couple test batches, the chocolate was just a bit overwhelming. For the pie to have a really lovely bite, the chocolate needed to be softened with cream so your fork can easily pull off a taste that melts in your mouth and complements the quinoa crunch.

Line an 8-inch springform pan with parchment paper.

In a medium bowl, melt the chocolate chips in the microwave, stirring every 30 seconds until smooth. (Alternatively, use a double boiler.) Add the cream and whisk until smooth. Pour half of the chocolate mixture into the prepared pan and spread it out in an even layer. Chill in the fridge for about 10 minutes, until hardened.

In a separate medium bowl, whisk together the peanut butter, agave, vanilla, and salt until combined. Add the puffed quinoa and fold to combine.

Remove the pan from the fridge and transfer the peanut butter mixture on top of the chocolate layer. Use a rubber spatula to pat the peanut butter into a flat, even layer.

Pour the remaining chocolate on top of the peanut butter and spread it out in an even layer. If you're making this in a colder climate, the chocolate mixture may harden before you add the second layer. Pop the bowl in the microwave for 20–30 seconds and whisk again until smooth.

Chill the pie in the fridge for about 30 minutes, until the top layer is hardened. Release the springform pan to remove the pie and transfer it to a cutting board. Cut into 8 slices.

I never knew icebox cakes existed until the day I saw Ina Garten make one on TV as I watched intently, mouth agape. I'm always down for easy, do-ahead desserts that are perfect for feeding a crowd, and icebox cakes fit the bill. This one is layered with thin chocolate cookies and a delicate strawberry whip that adds a touch of fruitiness to the rich chocolate. You can customize it and get creative. Bump up the amount of strawberry jam or nix it altogether and swap in peanut butter or Nutella. Once you have a basic icebox cake in your recipe arsenal, you'll be able to switch it up for any occasion.

Place the cream in a large bowl and use an electric mixer on high speed to whip for about 2 minutes, until the cream starts to stiffen. Add the cream cheese, jam, agave, vanilla, and food coloring. Continue to whip on high for 2–3 minutes, until stiff peaks form and the mixture resembles whipped cream.

Line an 8-inch springform pan with parchment paper. Arrange a layer of chocolate cookies across the bottom of the prepared pan. Feel free to fill any spaces between the cookies with smaller bits and broken pieces. Add a dollop of strawberry whip and spread it across the cookies in an even layer. Add another cookie layer on top, followed by a whip layer. Continue this process until all the whip is used, ending with a whip layer.

For a pretty, finished look, add more cookies on the top layer or crumble them over the cake. Chill the cake in the freezer for at least 12 hours, until set.

Release the springform pan to remove the cake. Cut it into 8 slices and enjoy.

Strawberry and Chocolate Icebox Cake

1 cup heavy cream

4 oz cream cheese, room temperature

½ cup strawberry jam

¼ cup agave nectar, honey, or pure maple syrup

1 teaspoon pure vanilla extract

2 drops red food coloring

1 box (about 9 oz) thin gluten-free chocolate cookies

MAKES 1 CAKE

PREP: 20 MINUTES +
12+ HOURS CHILL TIME

Hazelnut Affogato

One summer I studied in Rome for college credit and ate gelato every afternoon. A cup of hazelnut (nocciola) gelato in one hand, a small specialty gelato shovel spoon in the other. I fell in love after one bite and when I made this hazelnut-infused coffee and paired it with ice cream, it took me back to gelato breaks in Rome. Blending the nuts into the coffee allows your ice cream to swim in a super-creamy hazelnut pool, making for the perfect afternoon pick-me-up.

1 cup black coffee (hot or cold, depending on what you're feeling)

⅓ cup unsalted roasted hazelnuts

1 tablespoon agave nectar, honey, or pure maple syrup

Pinch salt

2 scoops ice cream of choice

SERVES 1

PREP: 10 MINUTES

Place the coffee, hazelnuts, agave, and salt in a blender. Blend on high until creamy.

Place a nut milk bag or clean, thin kitchen towel over a mug or bowl. Gather the edges and pour the liquid through the bag, squeezing all the liquid into the mug and leaving behind the pulp.

Serve warm in a mug with the ice cream, or serve cold by placing the ice cream in a tall glass and pouring the coffee over it.

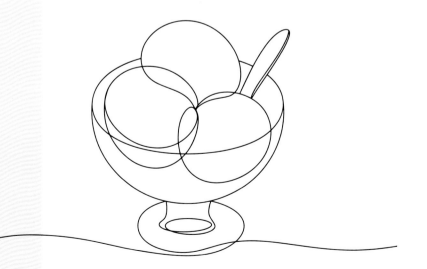

There's a restaurant on the boardwalk in Ocean City, New Jersey, called Bashful Banana that sells banana whips. When you put frozen bananas through a large juicer, they turn into a beautiful, luscious banana ice cream made from . . . just bananas! My cousins visiting from Indiana were bummed to leave their whips at the Jersey Shore, so they tracked down a second-hand industrial juicer and kept the whips alive. During the winter months, when the shore closed down, we began perfecting our own whips with a juicer. Then I invested in a high-powered blender with a tamper wand, which produced an unbelievably creamy nice (nana + ice) cream. You can finish it off with toppings like mini chocolate chips, fresh fruit, and granola.

Place the frozen banana pieces in a food processor or high-powdered blender with a tamper wand. Blend the bananas, stopping to use a rubber spatula or the tamper wand to move the banana pieces around to get them chopped up. Keep blending until the bananas are light, thick, and creamy.

In a small bowl, stir together the peanut butter and agave. Add the peanut butter mixture to the bananas and stir to create a swirl.

Scoop into 2 individual bowls.

Peanut Butter Swirl Banana Whips

4 bananas, cut into pieces and frozen

¼ cup natural peanut butter

1 tablespoon agave nectar, honey, or pure maple syrup

SERVES 2
PREP: 10 MINUTES

Sauces & Toppers

Because of my day job, I tend to have a lot of sprinkles on hand. There was a time when I rebranded some of my kids' food to make it more appetizing to their toddler palates. Yogurt was no longer just yogurt—instead we made special sprinkle yogurt. A banana wasn't just a mere lowly banana but became a party boat. Sprinkles elevated almost any dish, making it more fun, more special, and inevitably, more edible.

The magic of a sprinkle, a drizzle, or a crumble isn't lost on me. Adding that extra oomph on top is sometimes exactly what is needed to finish off a recipe and raise it from everyday to extraordinary.

Plus, it allows others to get in on the fun and customize their treat however they want. Add more crumble, drizzle more sauce, make it your own!

In this chapter, we're making everything from sauces and crumbles to glazes and toppers that will take any recipe up a notch.

Chocolate Chip
Cookie Crumble

Strawberry
Shortcake Crumble

Birthday Crunch
Crumble

Double Chocolate
Brownie Crumble

Peanut Butter
Cookie Crumble

Crumbles

These recipes are a nod to Christina Tosi's epic Milk Bar crumbles. They are perfect for topping your ice cream, cakes, or oatmeal—or eating straight with a spoon!

CHOCOLATE CHIP COOKIE CRUMBLE

MAKES 1 CUP

PREP: 5 MINUTES

½ cup natural cashew butter

¼ cup agave nectar

Dash pure vanilla extract

½ cup blanched almond flour

Couple pinches sea salt

½ cup chocolate chips of choice

Place the cashew butter, agave, and vanilla in a food processor. Process for about 15 seconds, until creamed together and combined. Add the almond flour and sea salt. Process again until the ingredients ball up.

Use a rubber spatula to scrape down the sides and process for another 5 seconds, until the ingredients ball up and are completely combined. Add the chocolate chips and process for 5 seconds, until they are incorporated into the dough.

Store in an airtight container in the fridge, or place in a bowl to enjoy immediately.

DOUBLE CHOCOLATE BROWNIE CRUMBLE

MAKES 1 CUP

PREP: 5 MINUTES

½ cup natural cashew butter

¼ cup agave nectar

Dash pure vanilla extract

½ cup blanched almond flour

2 tablespoons cocoa powder

Couple pinches sea salt

½ cup chocolate chips of your choice

Place the cashew butter, agave, and vanilla in a food processor. Process for about 15 seconds, until creamed together and combined. Add the almond flour, cocoa powder, and sea salt. Process again until the ingredients ball up.

Use a rubber spatula to scrape down the sides and process for another 5 seconds, until the ingredients ball up and are completely combined. Add the chocolate chips and process for 5 seconds, until they are incorporated into the dough.

Store in an airtight container in the fridge, or place in a bowl to enjoy immediately.

BIRTHDAY CRUNCH CRUMBLE

MAKES 2 CUPS

PREP: 5 MINUTES

¼ cup agave nectar

2 tablespoons unsalted butter

1 teaspoon pure vanilla extract

1½ cups blanched almond flour

½ teaspoon salt

½ cup puffed quinoa or crispy rice cereal

3 tablespoons rainbow sprinkles

In a large bowl, whisk together the agave, butter, and vanilla until combined. Add the almond flour and salt. Whisk until combined and a crumble forms. Fold in the puffed quinoa and sprinkles.

Store in an airtight container in the fridge and crumble on top of ice cream, cake, brownies, and more! Or roll into balls and enjoy.

PEANUT BUTTER COOKIE CRUMBLE

MAKES 1 CUP

PREP: 5 MINUTES

½ cup natural peanut butter

¼ cup agave nectar

Dash pure vanilla extract

½ cup blanched almond flour

Couple pinches sea salt

Place the peanut butter, agave, and vanilla in a food processor. Process for about 15 seconds, until creamed together and combined. Add the almond flour and sea salt. Process again until the ingredients ball up.

Use a rubber spatula to scrape down the sides and process for another 5 seconds, until the ingredients ball up and are completely combined.

Store in an airtight container in the fridge, or place in a bowl to enjoy immediately.

STRAWBERRY SHORTCAKE CRUMBLE

MAKES 2 CUPS

PREP: 5 MINUTES

2 oz freeze-dried strawberries

1 tablespoon salted butter, melted

1 tablespoon strawberry jam

½ cup puffed quinoa or crispy rice cereal

Place the strawberries in a food processor. Pulse for about 10 seconds, until the strawberries are crumbly. Add the butter and jam. Process again for 10 seconds, until the mixture begins to chunk up.

Transfer the strawberry mixture to a medium bowl and add the puffed quinoa. You can use a rubber spatula, but I like to use my hands to crunch the ingredients together and incorporate them.

Store in an airtight container in the fridge and enjoy on top of ice cream, yogurt, oatmeal, and more!

Ice Cream Shells

Chocolate shells were all the rage in my house in the late '90s. At some point, we bought a bottle of chocolate sauce at the grocery store that magically hardened when it hit the cold ice cream. We would all sit around and watch, eyes wide with amazement. The obsession grew a bit more intense when, a couple weeks later, we came home with a bottle that made a peanut butter shell. The transformation and excitement of breaking through the shell into the ice cream is something that has never left me. I was thrilled to learn years (decades?) later that chocolate (and peanut butter) behaved in a similar way when you stirred in some coconut oil. It's a super-simple kitchen trick to make an ice cream shell at home.

CHOCOLATE SHELL ICE CREAM TOPPER

MAKES 15 SERVINGS

PREP: 5 MINUTES

1 cup chocolate chips of choice

2 tablespoons refined coconut oil

In a small bowl, melt the chocolate chips and coconut oil in the microwave for about 2 minutes, stirring every 30 seconds to prevent burning. (Alternatively, use a double boiler.) Whisk until the ingredients are smooth and combined.

Spoon a tablespoon or two over ice cream. The chocolate shell will harden within a couple of minutes. To speed up this process, pop your bowl of chocolate-covered ice cream in the freezer. The chocolate can be stored in a glass jar in the fridge for up to 1 month. Separation may occur and that's okay. To use, simply reheat in the microwave or in a water bath on the stovetop, stir well and drizzle!

PEANUT BUTTER SHELL ICE CREAM TOPPER

MAKES 15 SERVINGS

PREP: 5 MINUTES

1 cup natural peanut butter

3 tablespoons refined coconut oil

In a small bowl, melt the peanut butter and coconut oil in the microwave for about 2 minutes, stirring every 30 seconds to prevent burning. (Alternatively, use a double boiler.) Whisk until the ingredients are smooth and combined.

Spoon a tablespoon or two over ice cream. The peanut butter shell will harden within a couple of minutes. To speed up this process, pop your bowl of peanut butter–covered ice cream in the freezer. The peanut butter mixture can be stored in a glass jar in the fridge for up to 1 month. Separation may occur and that's okay. To use, simply reheat in the microwave or in a water bath on the stovetop, stir well and drizzle!

Whipped Creams

I can't tell you how many times I've stood in front of a fridge with an upside-down can of whipped cream and dispensed it directly into my mouth. What? We've all done it! Do I still do it? Yes, but now I have even more ways to get my whipped cream fix! Homemade whipped cream is fun to customize with different flavors. Use it to decorate an icebox cake, dollop on top of hot cocoa, and anything in between.

CHOCOLATE WHIPPED CREAM

MAKES 10 SERVINGS

PREP: 5 MINUTES

2 cups heavy cream

¼ cup cocoa powder

¼ cup agave nectar, honey, or pure maple syrup

Place the cream in a large bowl. Use an electric mixer on high speed to whip until the cream begins to form soft peaks, about 3 minutes.

Add the cocoa powder and agave. Continue to whip on high until it has fluffy, firm peaks and resembles chocolaty clouds of happiness. This is best enjoyed immediately!

PEANUT BUTTER WHIPPED CREAM

MAKES 10 SERVINGS

PREP: 5 MINUTES

2 cups heavy cream

¼ cup natural peanut butter

¼ cup agave nectar, honey, or pure maple syrup

Place the cream in a large bowl. Use an electric mixer on high speed to whip until the cream begins to form soft peaks, about 3 minutes.

Add the peanut butter and agave. Continue to whip on high for about 2 more minutes, until the mixture stiffens to firm peaks. This is best enjoyed immediately!

Syrups, Compotes & Sauces

By now you may know that if I have the choice between a fruity syrup and a chocolate one, I'll be choosing the chocolate. But I believe in variety and diversity, so it only felt right to give you some fruity syrups to balance it all out. These syrups are divine on pancakes, muffins, ice cream, and even brownies. To switch up the flavor, swap in a different type of berry.

RASPBERRY SYRUP

MAKES ½ CUP

PREP: 5 MINUTES, COOK: 5 MINUTES

½ cup fresh or frozen raspberries

¼ cup agave nectar, honey, or pure maple syrup

1 tablespoon unsalted butter

1 teaspoon pure vanilla extract

¼ teaspoon salt

Place the raspberries, agave, butter, vanilla, and salt in a medium saucepan over medium heat. Bring to a boil and continue to cook, stirring frequently, for 5 minutes, until thickened and reduced.

If you love raspberry seeds and want a chunky syrup, enjoy as is. If you're a silky smooth kinda person, strain the seeds and pulp out and then drizzle the syrup on ice cream, cakes, muffins, oatmeal, and more. Store in an airtight jar in the fridge for about 1 week. Reheat in a water bath on the stove or in the microwave for easy drizzling.

STICKY CITRUS SYRUP

MAKES ½ CUP

PREP: 5 MINUTES, COOK: 20 MINUTES

2 large oranges

½ cup agave nectar, honey, or pure maple syrup

1 teaspoon pure vanilla extract

½ teaspoon arrowroot flour

Squeeze the juice from the oranges and pour it through a strainer to remove any pulp or seeds. You should have about 2 cups. Place the juice, agave, and vanilla in a small saucepan over medium-high heat. Bring to a boil, whisking frequently. Once bubbling, sprinkle in the arrowroot flour, whisking as you sprinkle so it doesn't clump. Continue to cook, whisking frequently, for about 20 minutes, until the syrup reduces and is stringy and sticky.

Transfer the syrup to a small jar with a spout to be drizzled on everything from pancakes to muffins, oatmeal, and more. The syrup is best enjoyed day-of but any leftovers can be stored in an airtight jar in the fridge for about 1 week. Reheat in a water bath on the stove or in the microwave for easy drizzling.

BLACKBERRY COMPOTE

MAKES ½–1 CUP

PREP: 2 MINUTES, COOK: 10 MINUTES

½ cup fresh or frozen blackberries

4 tablespoons salted butter

Juice of 1 lemon

¼ cup agave nectar, honey, or pure maple syrup

1 teaspoon pure vanilla extract

Place the blackberries, butter, lemon juice, agave, and vanilla in a small saucepan over medium-high heat, stirring frequently, stirring occasionally, until the glaze reduces, about 10 minutes. You still want chunks of blackberry so try not to break the fruit apart too much as you stir. If it ends up reducing too much, add some water to thin it out.

Remove the compote from the heat and transfer it to a small serving bowl. Spoon onto cakes, pancakes, muffins, oatmeal, yogurt, and more. This compote is best enjoyed day-of but any leftovers can be stored in an airtight jar in the fridge for about 1 week. Reheat in a water bath on the stove or in the microwave for easy drizzling.

GINGERBREAD SYRUP

MAKES ½ CUP

PREP TIME: 2 MINUTES, COOK: 5 MINUTES

½ cup coconut sugar

½ cup heavy cream

1½ teaspoons ground ginger

1 teaspoon ground cinnamon

½ teaspoon ground nutmeg

¼ teaspoon ground allspice

¼ teaspoon salt

Place the coconut sugar, cream, ginger, cinnamon, nutmeg, allspice, and salt in a small saucepan over medium-high heat. Bring to a boil, whisking occasionally. Once the mixture is boiling, continue to whisk frequently for about 5 minutes, until the syrup thickens.

Transfer the syrup to a small bowl or jar with a spout to be drizzled on all the things. This syrup is best enjoyed day-of but any leftovers can be stored in an airtight jar in the fridge for about 1 week. Reheat in a water bath on the stove or in the microwave for easy drizzling.

PUMPKIN SPICE SYRUP

MAKES ABOUT 1 CUP

PREP: 2 MINUTES, COOK: 10 MINUTES

½ cup coconut sugar

½ cup water

⅓ cup pumpkin puree

½ teaspoon pumpkin pie spice

¼ teaspoon salt

Place the coconut sugar, water, pumpkin puree, pumpkin pie spice, and salt in a small saucepan over medium-high heat, stirring frequently. Continue to stir for about 10 minutes, until the syrup thickens and reduces a bit.

Either spoon the syrup from the pan or transfer it to a bottle with a thin nozzle for easy drizzling. Drizzle it over vanilla ice cream, on pumpkin pie, or on top of your latte. This syrup is best enjoyed day-of but any leftovers can be stored in an airtight jar in the fridge for about 1 week. Reheat in a water bath on the stove or in the microwave for easy drizzling.

CHUNKY CHOCOLATE HAZELNUT SWIRL

MAKES 1½ CUPS

PREP: 5 MINUTES

½ cup chocolate hazelnut spread, such as Nutella

⅓ cup heavy cream

½ cup chopped roasted hazelnuts

In a medium bowl, whisk together the chocolate hazelnut spread and cream until combined. Add the hazelnuts. Whisk again until incorporated.

For a drippy sauce, you'll want to heat this up. Heat it in the microwave for 30 seconds or place in a small saucepan over medium heat and whisk until just heated through, about 5 minutes. Any leftover chocolate sauce can be stored in an airtight jar in the fridge for about 1 week. It may harden (which could be delicious to eat with a spoon!) but if you want to drizzle it, reheat in a water bath on the stove or in the microwave for easy drizzling.

BUTTERSCOTCH SAUCE

MAKES ABOUT ¾ CUP

PREP: 10 MINUTES, COOK: 5 MINUTES

½ cup coconut sugar

½ cup unsweetened coconut cream

4 tablespoons unsalted butter

1 teaspoon pure vanilla extract

1 teaspoon salt

Place the coconut sugar, coconut cream, butter, vanilla, and salt in a small saucepan over medium-high heat. Melt, whisking frequently, then bring to a rolling boil and continue to whisk for about 5 minutes, until the sauce reduces slightly.

Transfer the sauce to a small pourable container and enjoy on ice cream, homemade breads, and more. This sauce is best enjoyed day-of but any leftovers can be stored in an airtight jar in the fridge for about 1 week. Reheat in a water bath on the stove or in the microwave for easy drizzling.

HOT FUDGE SAUCE

MAKES 1½ CUPS

PREP: 5 MINUTES, COOK: 5 MINUTES

1 cup semisweet chocolate chips

½ cup heavy cream

2 tablespoons unsalted butter

Place the chocolate chips, cream, and butter in a small saucepan over medium heat. Cook, whisking continuously, until smooth, about 5 minutes. (Alternatively, microwave in a small bowl, stirring every 30 seconds until smooth.)

Spoon the sauce from the pan or transfer it to a bottle with a thin nozzle for easy drizzling. Drizzle it over vanilla ice cream, brownies, and more. This sauce is best enjoyed day-of but any leftovers can be stored in an airtight jar in the fridge for about 1 week. Reheat in a water bath on the stove or in the microwave for easy drizzling.

Acknowledgments

I wrote this book upon moving home to New Jersey after six years living across the country. Creating this book was a reflective and nostalgic time for me and allowed me to produce recipes that were (yes, delicious) but also acutely personal. This book, in many ways, is a homecoming back to my heart, my roots, myself.

It takes a village to bring a book to life and it wouldn't feel complete without appreciating the hard work, creativity, and tastebuds that went into making this book. I am so lucky and grateful to know and have worked with each of you.

To the readers of The Toasted Pine Nut, no doubt this book wouldn't exist without you. Thank you for sharing my love for sweet indulgences, for coming back for seconds, and for telling your friends and family about my recipes. I hope this book is always open on your counter.

A huge thank you to Amy Marr, who saw the vision we had for this book and rightfully decided there is always room for another dessert cookbook. Thank you for bringing this book into the Weldon Owen family.

Megan Sinead Bingham, you designed this book more beautifully than I could have ever imagined. Thank you for bringing these recipes to life in such an artful, lovely way.

Lorena Masso and Victoria Wollard, wow you knocked it out of the park! I love the colorful and dreamy moments you captured. People eat with their eyes first and I couldn't have asked for a better photo team to craft the images that bring readers to the table.

Leigh Eisenman, thank you for believing in my voice as an author and keeping me on track. I'm so happy we get to celebrate another cookbook together!

I'm so grateful to Jessica Reynolds-Cordon, who re-tested many of these recipes and provided thoughtful, meaningful feedback. You helped strengthen and elevate these recipes from across the pond, thank you.

To my mom Sharon, who generously shared her kitchen so I could develop these recipes. I fell in love with baking standing next to you, so it's only fitting the recipes in this book were created in your home. Thank you for always prioritizing dessert and allowing me to use the good knives at a questionably young age. I feel like it really boosted my kitchen confidence.

To my dad, Joe, whose love, hard work, and wisdom shaped who I am today. I couldn't be more grateful or proud to be your daughter. Thank you for your endless support and sprinkling in laughter whenever possible.

To my brother Cliff and his sweet family—my taste testers! It was so fun to have you swing by to grab a batch of treats. Thank you for lending your tastebuds to the creation of this book and championing my use of extra chocolate chips.

Jaryd, thank you for eating and gushing over all my recipes. Your husband goggles have given me the courage to reach beyond what I ever thought possible. Thank you!

I tend to save the best bite for last—Caleb and Nolan. You've both inherited my sweet tooth and I'll happily indulge in any dessert with you. I hope one day this book makes you smile in more ways than one.

Index

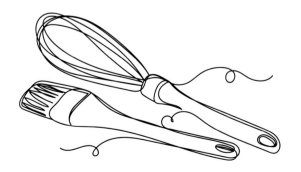

Something Sweet

Conceived and produced by Weldon Owen International

weldon**owen**

an imprint of Insight Editions
PO Box 3088
San Rafael, CA 94912
www.weldonowen.com

ISBN: 979-8-88674-013-4

Manufactured in China by Insight Editions
10 9 8 7 6 5 4 3 2 1

Weldon Owen would also like to thank Jessica Easto, Elizabeth Parson, and Sharon Silva.

Courtesy of Shutterstock:
anna_ku, page 160; Blinx, page 10; Ithile, page 170; Natalllenka.m, pages 119, 139, 146, 153; Olga Rai, page 4; Simple Line, page 77; Yanina Nosova, pages 26, 31, 44, 65, 69, 82, 89, 97, 103, 108, 122, 128, 143, 166, 173, 175, 188

CEO Raoul Goff
VP Publisher Roger Shaw
Associate Publisher Amy Marr
Editorial Director Katie Killebrew
Assistant Editor Kayla Belser
VP of Creative Chrissy Kwasnik
Art Director Megan Sinead Bingham
Production Designer Jean Hwang
VP Manufacturing Alix Nicholaeff
Production Manager Joshua Smith
Sr Production Manager, Subsidiary Rights
Lina s Palma-Temena

Photographer Lorena Masso
Food Stylist Victoria Woollard

Photo on page 177 taken by Monica Gomez

ROOTS of PEACE   REPLANTED PAPER

Insight Editions, in association with Roots of Peace, will plant two trees for each tree used in the manufacturing of this book. Roots of Peace is an internationally renowned humanitarian organization dedicated to eradicating land mines worldwide and converting war-torn lands into productive farms and wildlife habitats. Roots of Peace will plant two million fruit and nut trees in Afghanistan and provide farmers there with the skills and support necessary for sustainable land use.